Endorsements

"I've worked with the biggest of brands and TV personalities in the infomercial industry and have generated over $5 Billion in product sales in my career. I know the success traits necessary to make it in business. Brandon and Samantha got it! You are watching the launch of America's new generational leaders who are changing the way that you view and achieve success. I highly suggest reading *The Road to Success*!"

Kevin Harrington, Original Shark on ABCs *Shark Tank*,
Inventor of the infomercial

"To live an extraordinary life and be at the top of your game you must have a strong mindset and dedication to your mission. Brandon and Samantha resemble that on their journey with *Success in Your City. The Road to Success* shows you the necessary steps to achieve your biggest mission in life and how to find success in any endeavor you set out for."

Nick Lowery, Kansas City Chiefs Hall of Famer,
Keynote Speaker, Philanthropist

"*The Road to Success* is for anyone who is looking for more out of life and wants to learn from others who have found success in their own unique way. I highly suggest you read this book!"

Joel Comm, *New York Times* bestselling author and Founder of *Do Good Stuff*

"I got to work directly with Brandon and Samantha during the filming of the Scottsdale, AZ episode of *Success in Your City*. I've coached many entrepreneurs and business owners in my career, and it's always refreshing to experience the perspective of big thinkers like Brandon and Samantha! They aim high, act boldly and take massive action to move their dreams forward with persistence and grit! They show a way for others to also do what it really takes to achieve your biggest dreams, overcome obstacles, and keep moving forward with passion and heart!"

Mandi Monaghan, Co-Founder of The Monaghan Group Realty and Transformational Leadership Coach

"*The Journey of Success* is a brilliant documentation of getting out of your comfort zone and pursuing your passion. Brandon and Samantha are an inspiration to blaze your own path to Success. "

Shawn Vela, 13-Time Emmy Award-Winning Director, and Cinematographer

"I've traveled the world and have met with successful people from all walks of life. You can learn something from everyone's story. Brandon and Samantha share with you stories of success from individuals all over the country while also sharing their lessons learned in the process. This is a must-read for anyone who is looking for more out of life!"

Jeff Hoffman, Serial Entrepreneur from Priceline.com and uBid.com, Speaker, Philanthropist

The Road to Success

THE Road TO Success

How to Achieve Success in Business, Life, and Love

Brandon T. Adams & Samantha Rossin

NEW YORK

LONDON • NASHVILLE • MELBOURNE • VANCOUVER

The Road to Success

How to Achieve Success in Business, Life, and Love

Published in New York, New York, by Morgan James Publishing. Morgan James is a trademark of Morgan James, LLC. www.MorganJamesPublishing.com

ISBN 9781642798739 paperback
ISBN 9781642798746 eBook
Library of Congress Control Number: applied for

Cover Design by:
Chris Treccani
www.3dogcreative.net

Interior Design by:
Christopher Kirk
www.GFSstudio.com

Cover Photo by:
Rocky Nesta Media

Morgan James is a proud partner of Habitat for Humanity Peninsula and Greater Williamsburg. Partners in building since 2006.

Get involved today! Visit
MorganJamesPublishing.com/giving-back

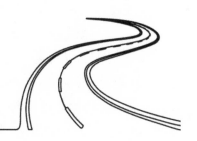

Table of Contents

Foreword by Kevin Harrington ix

Acknowledgments xiii

Introduction by Brandon T. Adams xix

Introduction by Samantha Rossin. xxxiii

Chapter 1:   Brandon T. Adams in Scottsdale, Arizona—Money,
              Power, and Fame Won't Make You Happy! 1
Chapter 2:   Samantha Rossin in Scottsdale—Giving Your
              Time to Others 17
Chapter 3:   Brandon in Austin, Texas—Faith, Love, and
              Never Giving Up 29
Chapter 4:   Samantha in Austin—The Power of Choice 41
Chapter 5:   Brandon—Accepting Change and Learning
              to Let Go. 55
Chapter 6:   Brandon in Boston—Networking Like Pros and
              Meeting Boston Ballers 65

Chapter 7:   Brandon—Giving Your Life Away for the Joy
             of Others 71
Chapter 8:   Brandon—Selling Everything and Our Next
             Chapter of the Show 83
Chapter 9:   Samantha in Denver—Your Story Matters 87
Chapter 10: Samantha—My Story Matters 103
Chapter 11: Brandon—Overcoming Obstacles 117
Chapter 12: Samantha—The Wedding in Nashville. 133
Chapter 13: Brandon—Life after the Show 147
Chapter 14: Brandon—The Road to the Emmys 159
Chapter 15: Brandon—The Netflix Journey. 165
Chapter 16: Brandon—Where Would We Be If We
             Didn't Pursue Our Dreams? 181

Afterthoughts from Brandon and Samantha. 185
Bonus Chapter: Kevin Harrington on Why Failure Is a
             Necessary Lesson 195
About the Authors 205

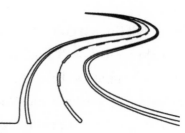

Foreword

By Kevin Harrington

I was fortunate enough to be born into a family of six kids and two parents. My father was a bartender and didn't have a lot of money. "When you grow up, Kevin," he said, "remember that you are number four. You gotta pay for your own high school, your own car, your own insurance, and your own college. Get ready. Buckle up. You gotta do it all on your own." I literally picked my high school, paid for it, had a car, moved out of the house when I was in high school, had my own apartment, and was making big money when I was a young kid. When I say "big money," I made as much as $1,000 per week on a good week—really good money back in the '70s.

My father had saved up some money so he could have his own business one day. He went from bartending to owning his own restaurants called Harrington's Irish Pub. I started working with him when I was just eleven years old. Doing this at a young age motivated me to become an entrepreneur. My dad helped that ambition along when he said, "You should be an entrepreneur, Kevin," and added, "I'm going to mentor you, but I'm not going to give you any money. Go do it! Go do it on your own! Figure it out!" So that's what I did. In my home city of Cincinnati, Ohio, I started a driveway-sealing business when I was fifteen. I then went on to start a heating and air-conditioning business. After selling that business, I started a brokerage company. This endeavor led me to create the infomercial business. Then boom! That led to billions of dollars in sales and becoming one of the original sharks of ABC's hit show *Shark Tank*. The success I had worked so hard for as a young entrepreneur all came together. I was seeing the results I had always envisioned when I was growing up.

In 1987, I and other young entrepreneurs started the Young Entrepreneurs Organization (YEO) to collaborate with and support one another's endeavors in business. As we got older, we changed our name to EO, the Entrepreneurs Organization. When I met Brandon T. Adams and heard what he was doing with the Young Entrepreneur Convention, I liked what I heard. Brandon reminded me of what I had done in my twenties as a young entrepreneur. I realized this was a new time where I could help him and also take myself and my business to the next level. So, I met Brandon, found he had a lot of great ideas, and told him I wanted to get involved with his effort. He wanted to start with conventions and creating content, such as video, podcasts, and more. After talking with him, I started to see that it's a different world of business out there today.

When I was a young entrepreneur, we didn't have the Internet and you couldn't create content. It was a whole different environment. Nowadays, I believe it's easier to be an entrepreneur. We didn't have twenty-one-year-old billionaires, like Kylie Jenner, who have a following on social media. Back in my day, I was starting heating and air-conditioning companies. Mark Zuckerberg was starting Facebook. Kylie Jenner is starting a billion-dollar cosmetic company.

What's the big difference today? There's more opportunity. I realized I needed to tune in to what these young entrepreneurs were doing. I missed the boat on digital when it first started. When all these young entrepreneurs were out there building followings and doing other amazing stuff, I decided I needed to be a part of it and that the best way to do that was to be involved with the young entrepreneurial community—with the Brandon T. Adams's of the world. That's why I got involved with Brandon and Samantha Rossin, Brandon's partner and wife—to be part of their business structure going forward with *Success in Your City*, a TV series. In their vision, I saw a lot of what I was doing back in the day, but what they are doing is on *steroids* with digital and utilizing this new world of Facebook, Instagram, and producing video content.

Getting involved with something from the beginning and tying your brand to it is very powerful. This is what I did when I got involved with *Shark Tank*, when it was in its beginning stages and had no TV distribution. *Shark Tank* is the idea of a great guy named Mark Burnett. I tied not only my own entrepreneurial abilities to it, but I wrote the check and invested in deals. I spent millions of dollars in investments in projects, even knowing that none of them might ever be seen by the television marketplace. Yet I believed in the *Shark Tank* concept and invested in it, and this has come to be one of the smartest things I've ever done.

That's another big reason why I wanted to get behind Brandon and Samantha's mission to create *Success in Your City*. They made the commitment to go all in on this show and now the same is true for this book you're holding—a book that will redefine the meaning of success and help you and others find your *own* meaning of success. Meanwhile, just like *Shark Tank*, Brandon and Samantha's TV show was just an idea with no TV distribution or even funding. That didn't stop them from pursuing their dreams and making this show a reality, traveling city to city, not even knowing where they were going to be living next. This show is an amazing commitment to the entrepreneurial world and the entrepreneurial spirit. I believe that entrepreneurship can be very powerful and very beneficial to the actual city itself. When a city has an area that starts transforming, this not only empowers local business owners to get involved with the change but it improves community spirit too.

As the executive producer of *Success in Your City*, I've witnessed Brandon and Samantha go on quite the journey the past few years pursuing this mission. They had some ups, they had some downs, and they overcame many obstacles in the process. In *The Road to Success*, you will read stories from their journey and, along the way, learn lessons from them. You will also learn from many different success stories they encountered and featured on *Success in Your City*, the TV show.

It's been an honor to be with them on this journey, to mentor them along the way in self-producing and hosting this show while they are also dealing with their own life experiences in the process. I've been there with them from the idea stage to the first day of shooting episode one to their season one finale, which falls on their wedding day in Nashville. It's been quite the ride! Brandon and Samantha have put the true meaning into living the American Dream and going after whatever you want. They never gave up and kept going until they reached the finish line. Now, you are about to read all about that journey in *The Road to Success: How to Achieve Success in Business, Life, and Love*.

Kevin Harrington
Inventor of the Infomercial and Original Shark
on ABC's Hit Show *Shark Tank*

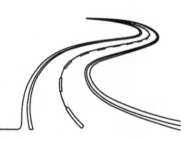

Acknowledgments

Thank you, Mom and Dad, for raising me to be the person I am today and for traveling with me on my entrepreneurial journey. Dad, I'm forever thankful for the lessons you taught me early on in business and for giving me the opportunity to become the spartan entrepreneur I am today. The ice business has helped me see that I can pursue anything I set my mind on.

Thank you to all my mentors who have guided me on this rollercoaster ride called life. It's a crazy ride and without all of you, I don't think I could have survived it. Thank you to my greatest mentor and inspiration, Napoleon Hill. We may not have met in this lifetime, but I know your spirit is with me. Your dedication to creating the success principles that humanity uses to further develop themselves in every aspect is a monumental accomplishment I could only hope to achieve. Your work has formed me into the person I needed to become in order to achieve any major success.

Thank you to my love, Samantha Rossin. I believe God had us meet for a reason, and I'm glad He did. You have influenced me to do things

I never thought imaginable. You picked me up when I was down, and you helped me keep things together when I felt like falling apart. I will always love you.

Brandon T. Adams

Thank you, Mom and Dad, for always being there for me. Through my teen years, I was an uncontrollable person who had no respect for either of you. I was living on my own terms, and I immersed myself in some scary situations. I wish I had understood that your concern for me came from a genuine place. For you guys to be there for me when I snapped out of the addiction world means so much to me. I wouldn't be where I am today without you. You guys have supported Brandon and me when we were broke, and you continue to support us by being our number one fans. You both have endless love for others, and with all of your responsibilities, you remain positive. I am honored to look up to you guys as role models and am blessed to have you as parents.

Samantha Rossin

So many people were part of the making of this book and TV show. We thank you all. If you aren't listed here, know that we are thankful for your support on our journey. The following people went above and beyond to support us.

The Success in Your City Team

Kevin Harrington

Jeff Hoffman

Shawn Vela

Mike Silvestri

Kai Honeck

Jeff Ottum

Carlos Medina

Jonathan Hickey

James Naleski

Thank you to the Keller Williams real estate community, which, through their individual teams throughout the country, made a huge contribution to fund our show.

Scottsdale, Arizona

Mandi Monaghan

Rich Barker

Michelle Schwartz

Scott Kiburz

Tom Ross

Andrew Zalasky

Shea Hillenbrand

Robin Orscheln

Glenn Pahnke

The Boys and Girls Club of Metro Phoenix

Jeremy Jones of FunkFit

Luis Galindo of FunkFit

Chris Lampkins

Chris Lo

Austin, Texas

Ricky and KodiKay Cain

Jackson Cain

The Cain Team

Cain Cares

Silvia Ward-Carden

Michael Ames

Sean Busse

Griffin Bruehl

Marvin and Melba Fein

Dave Haney

Riverbend Church

Johnny Beans Coffee

Gourdough's Donuts

Boston, Massachusetts

David France

Venture Café

Colette Phillips

Thaddeus Miles

Christopher Wolfel

Rhett Price

Tom O'Keefe

Samuel Thompson

The Roxbury Innovation Center

Devin Cole with WorkBar

Griffin Bruehl

Trung The Tran

Anastasia Dvoryanchikova

Josh Knowles

Kiyoshi Hayashi

Danny Koo

Denver, Colorado

Dan Gomer

Stephen and Katie Christopher

Marie Borquez

Jourdan and Kit Baldwin

Gerrad and Deirdre Brigham and Family

Joel Comm

Erin Cell

Brad Poppie

Nashville, Tennessee

Faydra Lagro

Brandon Green

The Bell Tower

Pine Street Flats

James Whittaker

Noah Anderson

Tiffany Davis

Peter and Chellanie Grunwald

Todd Cassetty

Brice Clark with Spark Events

Others

Andrew Zalasky

Greg Rollett

Chip Sullivan

Alex Bilodeau

Cactus Jack Barringer

Introduction by Brandon T. Adams

What is success?

That's a loaded question with many answers. One person's response to it may vary from another's. Success has many versions, and each is unique. Think about what success means to you. What is your version of success?

This question led Samantha Rossin and I on a journey across the country in 2018 to find the true meaning of success before tying the knot in marriage. This question and mission to find the true meaning of success led us to sell our home in Iowa, along with most of our material things. It led me to sell two of my companies, one of which had been in my family for more than thirty years. It led us to give more, love more, and sacrifice our own well-being at times to bring these stories to you through this book and our TV series, *Success in Your City*.

To say we are committed to your success is an understatement. We are determined to help you find your own version of success in life, and we believe the stories you are about to read will help you achieve that. Each story will teach you a valuable life lesson, and you may even see a bit of yourself in some of the people you will learn from. We are all very different but also very similar in ways. I personally saw a bit of myself in each of the individuals we spent time with during our tour across the country.

Before I give you a glimpse of all the success stories you are about to experience and learn from, I want to share with you what led us to ask the question about what constitutes success and to embark on this ambitious journey across the country.

Samantha and I had started out on this success journey together as a couple after we met in 2013. At that time, we were still figuring out who we were as people and what we really wanted in life. Samantha was finding her passion and what she wanted to do, and I was driven to find success in business and achieve goals such as earning large sums of money and accolades. I wanted to be known and respected by others. I wanted to prove my worth to the world by achieving something noteworthy. Along the way, I got caught up in the grind and lost focus in regards to Samantha. Ultimately, this led us to split up for ten months. This separation was one of the toughest times of my life, but it was also the best learning experience for the both of us. The time apart made it clear that we were meant to be together.

When we reunited in the fall of 2016, we had both found success in our careers. Samantha was a personal trainer and taught group training classes. I was running three companies while also filming the TV show *Ambitious Adventures* with Greg Rollett. At the time. I owned Adams' Ice Service, the business my father started in 1986, and I co-owned Keys to the Crowd, a crowdfunding consulting business, and the Young Entrepreneur Convention, an event to support young entrepreneurs. Additionally, I was working on the movie *Think and Grow Rich: The Legacy*, based on Napoleon Hill's classic best-seller *Think and Grow Rich*, which has sold more than 130 million copies worldwide.

Soon after getting back together, Samantha and I decided to move to Orlando, Florida. We both loved the weather there and felt like it was time to live in a new state to switch things up a little. I also wanted to be closer to my co-host, Greg Rollett, whose studio was in Winter Park, Florida. I knew if I wanted to take *Ambitious Adventures* seriously and get it out to the world, I needed to be close to Greg so we could work together regularly. Prior to moving to Florida, we had a TV distribution deal that would allow our show to be seen in forty million homes across America. Just two months after moving to Florida, that deal fell through and left us wondering what the next step was for our show. We had filmed season one and had planned on filming a second season.

While in limbo, I was forming a new company with my other co-founders of Keys to the Crowd. We saw market potential in becoming a leader in creating media content and helping others build their own brand online. I had built my brand as a crowdfunding expert and TV host, and I knew that I could help others build theirs. We formed the company Accelerant Media Group and started providing full-video production for entrepreneurs and business owners. We worked with the biggest of celebrities and entrepreneurs in building their brands, launching their products, and helping them monetize what they had already created in their careers.

While we were running Accelerant Media Group, I was investing a lot of time and money into my brand, specifically into video content. I hired my own videographer to follow me around and film with me every week, similar to what Gary Vaynerchuk does every day. Gary is a known Entrepreneur who owns VaynerMedia, a full-service digital agency and media company. He is known for creating daily video content. Gary's video guy was named DRock, but my guy was Herb Gonzalez. Together, we filmed with our clients, but we also filmed our own show called the *Live to Grind* show, which appeared on Apple

TV and Facebook. Together, we would travel city to city filming and working with clients. We filmed with some of the top influencers in the country and learned from their stories. We learned from millionaires, sharks, celebrities, professional athletes, and business owners who were in the top 1 percent of their industries. Not only were we getting paid to do what we loved, but we were learning from seasoned entrepreneurs and experts.

I became obsessive with producing video content while also learning from others. Each week, I would do two to three interviews for my podcast show, just so I could learn more from other people about success and life. My driver was the hunger to develop my mind and abilities in business. The one decision that really changed me as a human being was making the commitment to attend a self-development training course in Los Angeles called Mastery in Transformational Training (MITT). I spent three months in this training, which helped me discover what was holding me back in life. The training allowed me to be present in life and not always strive to achieve the next goal or make the next business deal. It also helped me become a better boyfriend to Samantha.

This training allowed me to look in the mirror and see who I really was and what I was doing in life. It gave me insight into my own motives and patterns. You see, many of us go through life doing certain things without even noticing that we are doing them. I realized I had spent my entire life working to succeed so I could prove to everyone I was worthy. Each one of my accomplishments had been another opportunity to prove my worth to Samantha, my family, my friends, my followers, and the mentors I looked up to. I was always seeking approval and worth. All of these people already saw me as worthy, but to me it was never enough.

Always seeking approval and self-worth stemmed from my childhood. I was born with a speech impediment. I had a lisp. As a kid, I was bullied and mocked because I couldn't speak like the other kids. I was different, which made me furious. I was angry that I couldn't speak like other kids. This drove me to figure out a solution and eliminate my speaking problem. Every single night, I practiced in front of the mirror saying "S,S,S,S,SH,SH,SH." Over time, my lisp went away, and I became better at speaking. By the time I got to high school, I no longer had a speech impediment.

I had not only been working to eliminate this impediment, but ultimately, I had been working to earn respect from others and show them my self-worth as a person. This experience in my early life formed my tendencies and desires to achieve success so I could gain others' approval. The desire for approval and showing my worth allowed me to achieve success in life through sports, competitions, businesses, and any goal I had set; but all of those accomplishments never truly fulfilled me.

Discovering this about myself was a true gift and if I hadn't discovered it, I'm not sure where I would be today. I probably wouldn't be married to Samantha, and I most likely would be chasing the next "high" of achievement, only to find out that it wouldn't fulfill my desire for happiness.

Are you someone who has had experiences similar to mine while growing up? Have they made you into a person who is always seeking approval and self-worth? If so, I'm sure they allowed you to achieve accomplishments in the public's eye, but are they really filling the need inside you or are they just a temporary fix?

In May 2017, I had just finished my training that had allowed me to unlock many things holding me back in life. I had also been on the grind nonstop for Accelerant Media Group. It was time for a vacation—for Samantha and me to get away. We needed a break from work and also time to really be together. We booked a trip to spend Samantha's twenty-eighth birthday in Puerto Rico. It was the beach, us, and no one else.

It was the first time in a while that I didn't have cameras on me; the first time in a while that I wasn't using my phone to produce video content for social media. We were there to relax and disconnect.

While sitting on the beach and drinking a piña colada, Samantha and I brainstormed ideas about what we wanted to do next in our lives together. What was going to be our next big adventure? We both had loved traveling together, which we had been doing since we first met. I mentioned the idea of traveling the country and living in different cities. I had read an article where Mark Cuban said you should live in five cities before you turn twenty-five. That article had stuck with me, and I had always envisioned traveling the country, experiencing different cities, and learning from others in those cities. Samantha and I went back and forth on ideas around this plan and what it could turn into. We realized if we really wanted to do this, we had to do it now, while we were still young. We knew if we didn't do it now, it might never happen. Later sometimes becomes never!

This conversation resulted in us deciding on the concept of living in twelve cities in twelve months and filming a TV show around our experiences so we could share what we had learned about success. As soon as we got back from our vacation, we started planning our trip. We needed to figure out how to fund it, and we also needed a dream team to help us carry out this mission. By August, we had our team in place.

The Dream Team

Shawn Vela. We knew we needed a director and cinematographer who would lead the filming of the show and its storyline. I had worked with Shawn on *Ambitious Adventures*, and we had gotten along well. Shawn became the director of the show Samantha and I were setting out to create. At the time he signed on to our idea, he had won five Emmy

Awards and had worked on some big projects that gave him the experience we were looking for.

Mike Silvestri. Mike was the cofounder of Accelerant Media Group and had been working with me since 2015. He created websites, loved working through the logistics of businesses (something I don't enjoy), and at times had been our therapist during the tough times in business. Mike became a producer and cofounder of the show Samantha and I were envisioning.

Kevin Harrington. To get taken seriously about our TV mission, we needed a big name behind our show. I had worked with Kevin on many projects, and we had built a great business relationship with each other. Kevin became our executive producer to give Samantha and me solid credibility and to open up doors for us, which we couldn't do alone. His network was massive, and he was well known for inventing the infomercial and for being the original shark on ABC's *Shark Tank*.

Jeff Hoffman. When you take on a big mission and start it from scratch, you need someone who has overcome many obstacles and seen massive success in business. I first built a relationship with Jeff when he spoke at my event, the Young Entrepreneur Convention. He was an amazing speaker and one of the wisest men I have ever met. Jeff is known for cofounding priceline.com and was a Hollywood producer for the movie *Cabin Fever*, which had a small budget of less than $1.5 million but went on to do over $100 million in revenue worldwide. He also had been on White House advisory boards. Jeff became our other executive producer to give feedback and valuable advice.

Many other amazing people helped us early on with creating the foundation of this show, but the professionals I just mentioned were the core people who started and stuck with us from start to finish.

After building our team and creating the foundation of what the trip and show would become, Samantha and I decided to do a mini-trip, which would be our test run for the twelve-month tour. On October 3, 2017, we started the mini-tour to visit some of the cities we planned on living in over twelve months.

Here are the original twelve cities on our list:

Scottsdale, Arizona

Austin, Texas

Denver, Colorado

Nashville, Tennessee

Kansas City, Missouri

Charlotte, North Carolina

Boston, Massachusetts

New York City, New York

Madison, Wisconsin

Salt Lake City, Utah

Portland, Oregon

San Francisco, California

During October, we made stops in these cities:

Des Moines, Iowa

Denver, Colorado

Vail, Colorado

Salt Lake City, Utah

Los Angeles, California

Santa Monica, California

Las Vegas, Nevada

Scottsdale, Arizona

This mini-trip was a great test for us and provided an inside look at what we could expect traveling together. We spoke at events and shared our message about the tour. In each city, we received feedback and ideas for our TV show concept. Some people were supportive, and some people were negative toward our mission. Some people told us that what we were setting out to do wouldn't work or thought we would need to give it more time to plan everything out. With any big idea, you will always have opinions and feedback. It's important to listen to others and hear what they have to say. You must also know when to take feedback into consideration and when to ignore it.

While in Los Angeles on October 13, 2017, I proposed to Samantha. She said yes, and I was the happiest guy on earth. During my own journey of success in business, life, and love, I had come to realize that the greatest success and value in my life was Samantha. She made me a better person, and she had been sticking with me for years during my entrepreneurial journey. Success wasn't the same without her, and that's exactly why I wanted to marry her. She had completed my life and made it better. In my mind, love is the most powerful thing we have as humans. The love you have for your significant other will flow into other areas of your life. That love will drive your business and other endeavors you set out to engage in. Love has driven me to heights I couldn't have reached alone.

The day after proposing to Samantha, we attended the movie premiere for *Think and Grow Rich: The Legacy*, the movie I was a producer of and also featured in. This premiere was one of the highlights in my career up to that point because Napoleon Hill's book *Think and Grow Rich* had made such a positive impact on me when I read it six years before. I could go on for days about the power of the book, but I will let you read it for yourself to understand firsthand what I'm talking about. Meanwhile, what I'm about to share with you is probably one of the most pivotal moments early on for our journey with *Success in Your City.*

During the premiere, Samantha and I had a conversation with Mandi Monaghan and Michelle Schwartz, who were there to watch the *Think and Grow Rich* movie for the first time. Mandi was a new friend of mine who had joined my mastermind coaching program five months before, and Michelle was her guest. Samantha and I shared with these two women more about our vision for our trip and what we were setting out to do with *Success in Your City*. Mandi and Michelle heard our enthusiasm loud and clear and saw our vision. So, they volunteered to put on a VIP dinner for Samantha and me in Scottsdale, Arizona, so we could share our vision of the show and how others could get involved. Scottsdale was our first city on the twelve-city tour, so this was a great first step toward making connections that could help us.

Two weeks later, we were in Scottsdale at that VIP dinner. That dinner led to obtaining the sponsorship money for the first city and also led us to land our featured story for episode one of *Success in Your City*: Shea Hillenbrand.

This experience taught us that you should always share your vision with others and do it with enthusiasm and passion. That thirty-minute conversation with Mandi and Michelle at the premiere turned into the connections and funding for two of the cities on our tour. You never know when an opportunity will come your way. The way to land more opportunities and be in the right place at the right time is by always showing up in life. The more you show up, the luckier you will get. Since the VIP dinner in Scottsdale resulted in a big success, we made it our last city on the mini-tour and went back to our home in Iowa to start planning the real tour for 2018.

After several months of planning, we were ready to start our one-year tour. We felt as ready as we would ever be. On December 27, 2017, we left our home in Iowa at minus-seven degrees and started our drive to Scottsdale to embark on our journey for *Success in Your City*.

You are about to experience the twelve months of our lives and others' lives we encountered during this trip around the country. You will experience the ups and downs Samantha and I experienced while pursuing this mission, and you will see how our version of success changed along the way.

You are going to learn about unconventional success stories from individuals who are no different than you and me. Each story will show a lesson learned about success in business, life, or love, or maybe all three. Each person we spent time with and featured on our show had overcome obstacles to become who they are today. We learned something different from each success story and each city that we lived in. Samantha and I will share with you our own perspectives about what we learned and how we viewed success differently along the way. What you take away from these stories may not be the exact same thing we took away, but that's alright. What matters is that your takeaways and lessons will help you figure out what success means to you and how you can achieve it. Maybe you think you know what it is, but it could very well change along the way.

In Scottsdale, you are about to learn how a two-time MLB All-Star went from making $20 million in his career to leaving the game and eventually losing it all and living out of his van. We will share his lessons learned on and off the field and how he got out of the van and onto stages as a motivational speaker.

In Austin, you will learn how a real estate couple went from sweeping floors and having their office in a closet to building a real estate empire that is selling and renovating homes in need with a nonprofit they established. You will also learn the power of faith, love, relationships, and giving back to others.

In Boston, you will learn how a guy went from being homeless, sleeping on the streets at night, to creating an award-winning orchestra for youths and becoming a TEDx speaker, inspiring lives all around the world. You will learn how he has built real connections in business and life and how you can create your own connections by adding value to others.

In Denver, you will encounter women in the fitness arena sharing their rough obstacles in life and how they used their past to fuel them to become stronger in and out of the gym. Each of their stories will show you that anything is possible if you put your mind to it. Samantha will go into the details of her own experiences in Denver and the story of her past. She even calls off our wedding while in this city.

In Nashville, you will learn how a country singer risked it all to pursue her dream of playing on a main stage and having others hear her music. Her journey will show you what's possible when you go all in on your dreams and do not let others tell you otherwise. While in this city, you will hear the planning behind our wedding and how Samantha pulled it all off.

You will learn more about Samantha's story of overcoming drug addiction at fourteen years old and how she survived an eight-year abusive relationship that controlled her entire life. Eight years later, she has become an Emmy Award-winning producer, TV host, and coauthor of this book, while also empowering other women to become truly happy with who they are.

These are just some of the powerful stories Samantha and I will tell in this book. You are soon going to find out that success might not be what you think it is. Most of society will tell you that it is based on money, power, and fame. These stories will give you a different perspective on success.

You are also going to see inside Samantha's and my life during the journey traveling across the country and filming our TV series. The experiences we will share have never been shared, until now.

By the end of this book, you should be able to answer these three questions:

What is my version of success?
What does it take to get there?
What does it take to keep it?
Your success journey starts right now!

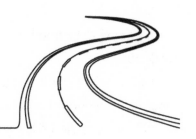

Introduction by Samantha Rossin

Alright, so let me just lead off from all of Brandon's accomplishments into my life, which is quite different. Haha! Thanks, babe, for making me feel like I need to make up a million things to get on your level. Just kidding. Good thing my accomplishments make me who I am, someone I am proud of, so being just like you isn't a goal.

As Brandon mentioned, we met in 2013. I had been living in Orlando at the time and was home in Winona, Minnesota, for a running relay with some friends. I had also just gotten out of an eight-year relationship that, unfortunately, had left me depressed and at my lowest. I had gone out on the town in Winona after accomplishing the running relay and decided to get drunk as hell to cover up all the hurt from the split with my ex. I used alcohol to hide the pain, and this night was no different. Brandon was in my hometown on his annual river trip with his friends, and I bumped into him at one of the local bars. I pushed my way into his group, had him buy me a shot, exchanged numbers, and left knowing I would never see him again. Dating was not on my mind, and I definitely wasn't going to be finding my future husband in a bar. Funny how things work out.

I flew back to Orlando the next day, and Brandon and I found each other on Facebook. I creeped on him so hard trying to remember what he looked like. We ended up texting each other and Skyping for three months. I had never been so close to someone, yet so far away. I told him everything. I told him that I was once a meth addict at age fourteen. I told him that I had just left my ex, who treated me poorly. I told him I didn't have a car or a college degree. The craziest part was that he still continued to talk to me. He saw past what I didn't have and appreciated what I did have. Well, okay then. *Who is this guy? Why did we end up at the same exact bar at the same exact time, and how did I give him my number out of the hundreds of guys around?* The whole situation awed me, but I didn't think we would ever end up dating. Fast forward to November of the same year, and he was moving me back to the Midwest, where we started dating.

I was still in the midst of finding who I was. I didn't have a career nor any passions that I was excited to pursue. I was just trying to understand life and how I could overcome such a sad part of it. As I watched Brandon work extremely hard, I wanted to do the same. I wanted to wake up every day and work toward building a better life for myself. Shortly after we started dating, we moved to Des Moines, Iowa, and he promised me a full-time job with the new company he was going to start called Adams Product Innovation. I felt like it was a good opportunity, so I agreed to join him. We worked on the business plan and soon came to realize that it wasn't going to work. He had our entire lives laid out and, in an instant, it was taken away. I became upset as we had no idea how we were going to pay for the rent on our brand-new apartment downtown.

What could I do to help us? I hadn't gone to college. I was so stuck on what I should focus on to become happy. We ended up joining a gym, and it hit me: personal training. I had always had a passion for lifting weights and running. I could definitely see myself helping others in that way. Fitness started to become a huge reason why I kept looking forward to life instead of looking back. I used the obstacles to fuel my workouts. I used my pain to prove to myself that I was stronger than I thought. I spent hours and days studying for the personal training certification, and on December 31, 2015, I passed my exam and started a new journey.

I spent a couple of years training at different gyms. I always tried to get outside my comfort zone, so I started my own in-home training company, SR Fitness. I was so passionate about helping people find time to move their bodies. I remained in the fitness industry until about 2017 and decided to put that passion on hold to pursue *Success in Your City*. I still stayed active and was always giving advice, but I knew that I needed to focus primarily on the show so that Brandon and I could make it superimpactful. Man did I get myself into an emotional journey. If I had known the type of obstacles we were going to encounter over the next twelve months, I would have never committed to the show; but because I did live it, I came out a completely different person and learned the most important things about myself and how I'm the only one in charge of my own happiness. I'll let you read about the differences between Brandon and me and what we accomplished to really understand what it takes, generally speaking, to go after something much, much bigger than yourself.

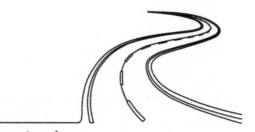

Chapter 1
Brandon T. Adams in Scottsdale, Arizona

Money, Power, and Fame Won't Make You Happy!

Living in a Mansion

On December 27, 2017, Samantha and I packed our Tahoe full of our bags and the stuff we thought we needed for our tour, then we made our way toward Scottsdale, Arizona. The moment we left for our trip across the country was unexplainable. We were nervous and excited about what lay ahead. There were many unknowns and many questions we had yet to answer, but we were on a mission to figure things out and go all in on this journey together. Forty-eight hours later, we pulled up to a mansion in Scottsdale, where we were going to live during our stay. Literally hours before getting into the city, a local real estate agent had confirmed that the owners of the mansion would allow us to stay in it. We had bartered with them for the stay in return for a promotional video of their house to help them sell it.

We pulled our Tahoe into the three-stall garage and walked into the mansion to discover what our home would be like for the next six weeks. It was way bigger than we had imagined. It gave me this instant feeling of accomplishment or sense that "we made it." We were about to spend the next six weeks in a $3.2-million-dollar mansion with four bedrooms, four bathrooms, a huge kitchen and living room, and a pool in the backyard. The house had a perfect view of Camelback Mountain and the most beautiful sunrise I had ever seen.

It took a few days of living there to adapt to our new temporary home. Being in such a big house with just the two of us was a bit creepy. During the first few days, the hot-water heater didn't work, so we had to shower in freezing-cold water. Not having hot water to shower in gives you a great appreciation for the simple feeling of having a hot shower. I learned to be thankful for the little things in life, such as a roof over my head, a hot bath, and a home-cooked meal. Since the house was so new, we were afraid to use the oven. We didn't want to make anything look used. We also cleaned the place religiously in case an unexpected showing of the house were to happen. Soon, Samantha and I found out that living in such a big house wasn't as awesome as we had imagined it to be.

My Birthday Experience

We spent our first few days in Scottsdale adventuring and having fun. One of our show sponsors had given us free tickets to a college bowl game, so our first Saturday in the city, we watched football. The next day was December 31—my twenty-eighth birthday. Samantha woke me up before sunrise and surprised me with the challenge to climb Camelback Mountain for the first time. The climb wasn't easy, but after a few hours, we made it to the top just in time to watch the sunrise. I experienced an amazing feeling of accomplishment. This was a great start to our journey together around the country. We looked over the city and surrounding areas with no worries in the world. It was a peaceful time together before our real challenge would commence.

It was our last day before having to get to work to figure out how we were going to pull off the first filming dates, which were only fifteen days away. Many unknowns loomed ahead. How would things go filming with Samantha? Yes, I had filming experience from my past TV show, *Ambitious Adventures*, but Samantha and I had very little experience filming with each other. Additionally, we still needed to find our filming locations, the talent for scenes, and to finalize the first episode's storyline. Another concern: our finances. We had raised money from sponsors to film the first episode, but the filming costs and travel for our crew were starting to become way more than we had anticipated.

When we first set out to travel the country and do the series, we had to find funding and sponsors along the way. Additionally, we had no distribution deal with a network. Most people shoot a pilot for a TV concept, pitch it to the networks, and hope to land funding to film a series of episodes. We did the complete opposite! No normal person would try to do what we did because they would've thought it was impossible, due to lack of funding. Samantha and I, on the other hand, had the "build it, and they will come mentality." We always kept moving forward as if things would just fall into place, and they always did, at least up to this point in our journey.

The Work Begins

New Year's Day came, and our 2018 journey had begun. We were about to have an experience of a lifetime that was unlike any we could have predicted. At the mansion, we held a group meeting with our sponsors and Shea Hillenbrand, who we would be featuring in episode one. The sponsors of the Scottsdale episode not only helped fund it but they gave us introductions, helped us find locations to film, and worked with us to help Shea with his career transition, which I'll touch on a little later. Our first meeting was very collaborative and resulted in us creating a fundraiser for the Boys and Girls Club in Metro Phoenix. Shea had built a baseball field for the Boys and Girls Club years before, and one of the sponsors had a strong connection with the club, which made it a perfect fit. One of the main objectives in each city was to give back in some way, and this was our way to contribute to a great cause. We had only two weeks to prepare for the fundraiser.

If we didn't have the sponsors working with us in the first city, I have no idea how we would have been able to pull off the fundraiser and film week. Everyone came together to support this cause and supported Shea throughout the process. It's not an easy task being featured on a TV show. Shea had to be available to film four days straight, and there were many emotions that he experienced while he told his story on camera. Sharing your story with the world can bring out another side of you. Throughout the year, we would find out that every single person we filmed had some kind of inner emotion they had to deal with and conquer while on set. Also, each individual sharing their story on camera had to put a lot of trust in the cameraman and editor, because they are the ones interpreting their story and message for a large audience. In reality TV, sometimes producers portray the story the way they want to portray it with the main focus being to gain more viewers, sometimes at the expense of the talent's reputation. Our team wasn't like that at all. Our goal was to always stay true to the person's story and share the story that would make the biggest positive impact on others' lives.

Filming Begins

On Monday, January 15, our film crew flew into Arizona to start filming episode one. We had been working toward this week since the idea had come about on that beach in Puerto Rico. I was excited but also nervous about how the week would turn out. We had many people relying on us to capture a great story for the show, and a few days away we had another event planned. People would be flying in to attend it from all over the country. I was also nervous for Samantha. It was her first time being filmed for a TV show, and, as much as possible, I wanted to help her be comfortable on camera. I also wanted Samantha to feel like she was a big part of the show and mission because up to this point, she had questioned her worth and purpose on this mission. Many of our sponsors and people we met in the city didn't give her the attention she deserved and thought she was just there, along for the ride. That was far from the truth. Samantha always gave her wisdom at the right time. She didn't talk as much as me and didn't put herself out front and center, but when she did provide wisdom, it was monumental to our success. She is a wise and strong woman. This is what I love about her most.

The first few days on camera together were a learning curve for Samantha and me, but after a while, we found our rhythm. Our director, Shawn Vela, was a great coach for Samantha and brought out the best in her. He brought out the best in all of us. Shawn helped craft the narrative in a way that told a powerful story and gave the viewer an inside look into our lives and personalities individually and as a couple. The main purpose of the episode was to share Shea's success story and show his journey in achieving it. The episode also showed how we perceived Shea's story and how it made us look at success differently.

The Shea Hillenbrand Story

Shea Hillenbrand had spent most of his childhood and early adulthood playing baseball. That was all he knew. It was his identity. To make it to the major leagues, you have to dedicate your life to the sport, and even then, you aren't guaranteed a spot on the team. It takes pure persistence and showing up on and off the field. Baseball had consumed his life and made it hard to spend quality time with his family. During his seven-year Major League Baseball career he played for the Boston Red Sox, Arizona Diamondbacks, Toronto Blue Jays, San Francisco Giants, Los Angeles Angels of Anaheim, and the Los Angeles Dodgers. He became a two-time All-Star and accumulated $20 million during his career. He was one of the best-known players of his time. Many thought he had it all, but in reality, Shea got tired of playing baseball and wasn't fulfilled. In 2007, he made one of the biggest decisions of his life to leave the game at his prime and go spend more time with his wife and kids.

Shea had experienced the life of money, power, and fame. Large crowds cheered for him, and he had achieved his childhood dream of playing Major League Baseball. His career highlights were hitting a game-winning home run off of Mariano Rivera, having three home runs in three consecutive innings, and being an All-Star player in 2002 and 2005. Despite all of those accolades, he wasn't fulfilled or happy. Something was missing. He left baseball and pursued his second childhood dream of owning a zoo. Four years later, his fifteen-year marriage fell apart, he received the third foreclosure notice on his farm, and everything else in his life was rattling out of control. He lost everything.

Shea found himself parked outside of his wife's house sleeping on the floor of his van. After taking fifteen sleeping pills, eight ibuprofen 800s, and downing countless drinks of alcohol, he asked the Lord to take his life. Here was a guy that everyone envied and looked up to, while Shea was unfulfilled, suicidal, and full of guilt and shame. He had hit rock bottom.

The next day when Shea woke up and had nothing left, he believed God had spoken to him. That was the first time he experienced this. God told him to pick up his cross and follow him. Shea's first thought: *Where is my horse?* When he thought about his old horse, he felt good. His horse had been sold months before, when he lost his farm, but he reached out immediately to find his faithful companion. He believed

God had put that thought in his mind for a reason. He wound up meeting with the woman who had bought his horse. Eventually, that woman became his wife, who he is with and loves dearly to this day.

She supported Shea in his transition, kept him accountable, loved him, and lifted him up. Shea had all of the things that most people would think would make you happy, but they meant nothing to him. He found happiness through having a relationship with God and his relationship with his wife. All of this led him to do what makes him most happy, which is speaking to, and inspiring, others. He started speaking in churches, prisons, and schools to share his message of going against all odds and overcoming obstacles. He thought baseball was his thing, but in reality, speaking was his real passion. Speaking fulfilled him and made him happy.

To start, to go against all odds and overcome them was how he became a two-time All-Star in the Major Leagues. Shea should never have made it—he recognized that he had been a serious underdog. That knowledge also filled him with the desire to help the underdog because everyone has a story and a purpose, and he wanted to help people overcome the serious odds against them. Shea believes that when you align your will with God's will, you can go against all odds.

What We Learned from Shea's Story

Shea made us realize that you can have all the money, power, and fame in the world and still not be happy. Shea's transition out of baseball was difficult, like most professional athletes experience when they leave a sport. Their life and identity are caught up in the game and once they leave it, they don't know what to do next. They don't know how to act or fit in with society. This isn't just the case for sports, but it also relates to people working at the same company for decades or building a company and selling it. Once they leave that company or position, they find it difficult to transition. It's important to not let your entire identity get caught up in one thing because when it's no longer in your life, it may get the best of you.

Our Core Mission in Scottsdale

We had four core objectives while in Scottsdale:

Learn about success from the community and Shea's story.

Give back to the community in some way.

Help Shea with his speaking career.

Capture the best story on camera to inspire and motivate as many people as possible.

During filming, we captured many scenes that highlighted Shea's story, gave an inside look into Samantha's and my life while in the city, showed Samantha and me helping Shea become a speaker, and showed the process of raising money for the Boys and Girls Club.

One of the most difficult scenes to capture was Samantha and me climbing Camelback Mountain. This time, it was for the show and not my birthday. This wasn't put in the script or shooting schedule; it was a last-minute decision our team made twenty-four hours before shooting. Samantha wasn't too fond of the decision. Halfway up the mountain, we got lost in the dark and started walking on the wrong trail. It was very cold, and Samantha thought her fingers were getting frostbite (a bit of exaggeration on her part). It also didn't help that she hit her knee on the way up and said she wanted to go back. I felt bad for her, but I also didn't want her to give up on herself by quitting. We kept going and eventually made it to the top. We got an epic drone shot, and she was glad I had pushed her to keep going.

Sometimes in a relationship, you have to push your significant other and hold them accountable, even when they tell you they don't want to do something. We never forget moments like these. Climbing

Camelback again was one of the most difficult things we had to do to get one shot for the show. It may have just been a ten-second shot, but it was the shot that made the scene. At times during film week, we were tired, getting by on two to three hours of sleep, but we still gave it our all and showed up on camera as if we were full of energy. We had to. It wasn't like we could reshoot on another day, especially with our budget. We had to make the timeline and our schedule work, even when we got delayed. Some days, we filmed sunrise to sunset. Without our film crew's hard work and dedication, we never could have pulled off the shoot. Any other production team would have taken seven days for the amount of footage we captured in four days. Success was our only option for filming, and we made it work. We discovered that when we were pushed to figure things out, we always figured them out. Sometimes it felt like it was going to be impossible to pull off a scene, but we always managed to do it.

The Boys and Girls Club and the Fundraiser

Besides the few weeks we had to plan for the filming, we also had to plan an event to raise money for the Boys and Girls Club. In addition to holding the event, we were going to film it for the show, which made the task more tedious.

Prior to the fundraiser, Samantha and I spent some time at the Boys and Girls Club of Metro Phoenix to meet with the kids and see if we could help in any way. The Boys and Girls Club is a place for kids and young adults to go after school. Many of the kids have difficult situations at home and may not want to be there. They may not have parents, they could be in a poor family or a troubled family, or they could even be in a situation where the people around them are gang members or drug dealers doing things that could lead them to jail or even being killed.

Samantha and I connected with three teenagers who really caught our attention. We fell in love with them right away. They all had obstacles but also had dreams and visions to do more after high school. During film week, we both attended the club and filmed various scenes with the kids. Until the day I die, I will never forget one specific scene. Most likely it will not be seen in the show to protect the confidentiality of the individual's personal story. At any rate, it stuck with me because during the shooting of the scene, I had one of the kids in tears while the other two were blown away by what I had said to them. I learned more about their stories and asked them questions to get a better idea about their backgrounds and how I could give them the best advice to improve their lives and push them to go after their dreams. I won't share the specific feedback that I gave them, but I will share the core takeaway, which is what all kids should hear at a young age.

I told each of the kids that they could achieve anything if they really put their minds to it. I told them that if they work hard, surround themselves with the right people, and show up in their lives in a positive and consistent way, they would be able to achieve amazing things. This seems like regular advice any self-help guru would give to you, but these kids had not heard that enough in their lives. It's as simple as saying, "You can do anything you set your mind to." Those nine simple words can change someone's life, especially when you hear them at a young age. Hearing this encouragement when a person is young can build up a mindset and thought process of success versus a limited mindset that doesn't see beyond a current situation.

Today, many parents tell their kids that they need to get good grades, go to college, get a degree, and work a safe job for the rest of their lives. I don't disagree with the good grades or college degree (depending on the situation), but I do think that kids need to have more ability to think on their own in school. I believe they should be taught that there are other paths to take that don't just consist of going to college or working the nine-to-five grind. We now live in a world that allows you to be free, travel, work from home, and be a person of influence without having a college degree.

The kids at the club didn't have the type of childhood I had growing up. I had loving parents who gave me direction and ensured I kept my focus on sports, hunting, and other things that kept me away from gangs or drugs. This made me realize how lucky I was as a youth but also how many parents need to make some changes on how they raise their kids. How a child is raised from birth to age eighteen will, ultimately, determine how their lives will turn out. I loved the Boys and Girls Club so much because they were giving these kids a chance to make it in life, because in some cases their home lives were not setting them up for success.

Spending time with the kids prior to the fundraiser gave Samantha and me the desire and motivation to raise as much money as possible for the club. We settled on four main ways to generate revenue for the fundraiser: event ticket sales, VIP tickets to attend a mastermind with Kevin Harrington, live paddle bidding, where people would raise their paddle for the amount of money they wanted to donate, and an auction of items, such as time with Shea, Kevin, or myself to help with a business. Since Kevin is a good friend and also the executive producer of our show, he donated his time as a speaker for the event, which helped us sell tickets.

Fundraiser day arrived, and we were as ready as we were going to be. The event didn't start until four p.m., so beforehand, we spent the day filming for the show. Our sponsors and Scottsdale mentors worked at the venue to prepare for the event the entire day while we filmed. The event would be held at the actual Boys and Girls Club of Metro Phoenix, which would give attendees an inside look at the club. Late that morning, Kevin Harrington had flown in to be in a scene we had for the show, which involved Kevin, Shea, and me playing a round of golf. During this scene, Kevin gave Shea feedback on his speech he was going to give that night and helped prepare him for the fundraiser. Just a few hours before the fundraiser, we wrapped up filming, then we changed quickly and made our way to the Boys and Girls Club.

We were on a mission to raise as much money as possible so we could give a large check to the club. Since I had a background in raising money for charities, I believed we could raise a lot of money during the night. If you ever want to put on your own charity fundraiser, here are my four main tips for success:

1. **Create an experience for the event attendees.** Serve hors d'oeuvres and drinks, play music, and make sure that VIPs are in the room. They could be local celebrities, people who are known for their work, or anyone of influence. These kinds of people will attract others but will also put everyone into a higher frequency level of thought and energy that will make the event a bigger success.

2. **Provide value to the attendees.** You must give value before you can ask for it in return. In this case, we were asking for donations for the club. Besides the food and drinks, we provided the attendees with knowledge from amazing speakers, who we would eventually auction off at the end of the night. The attendees got to see what knowledge and value the speakers had to offer before they had the chance to bid on us.

3. **Show exactly where the money is going.** Many people are trying to raise money for their own charities. People are getting hit up every single day. To get others to support your charity of choice, you must show them why yours stands out from the rest. You must show the emotional story behind it and why money is desperately needed. Before starting the auction, we had one

of the employees come up and share their experience working with the kids at the club and how he personally had attended the club as a kid. He shared the impact it had on his life. This was a real-life testimonial for the audience to demonstrate to them how powerful the program is and what their money would be funding. In hindsight, we should have also featured a kid who is currently in the program talk about it. If we had, I'm confident we would have raised more money.

4. **Have an experienced auctioneer.** The auctioneer will help you determine how much money you can get for auction items. We were lucky to have an experienced person who had performed many charity auctions. His name is Bobby D. of Call to Auction. He also helped us raise lower donation amounts from all of the attendees, from $25 to $250. He engaged the crowd and made them comfortable to raise their paddles for various donation levels. There is a science and system behind this. When you have the right auctioneer, your fundraising event will soar to another positive level.

The event became a huge success. Every speaker did an amazing job in providing value to the attendees, and Shea Hillenbrand gave a damn good keynote address! We had been working with him in the weeks leading up to the event, and he delivered his speech even better than I could have imagined. We had success with our larger ticket items too. The top two items auctioned were time with me and time with Kevin. Kevin Harrington donated an hour for a one-on-one in-person meeting, which resulted in a $5,000 donation to the club. I donated a half day of consulting and filming with me, which resulted in a $5,000 donation. Just from the two of us donating our time, we raised $10,000. The final total, which we raised from ticket sales and the auction that night, was close to $40,000. After hearing the final number, I cried tears of joy.

That we had all come together and used our resources and collaboration to raise that much money in just two weeks had blown me away. It reminded me what type of results can be created when you bring people together to work toward a common goal, which in this case was to raise money for the Boys and Girls Club.

Final Thoughts about Our Time in Scottsdale

The fundraiser and event became a big success, but our week was not over. We still had to wake up early the next day to film more show scenes, and we needed to film some extra content with our sponsors. One of the perks we gave to the sponsors of the Scottsdale episode was an on-camera interview of them talking about their business and sharing their own version of success. It was interesting to hear each sponsor's experience about how this filming and fundraising had positively impacted them. Everyone felt a sense of fulfillment from what we had accomplished together. All of us had worked as a team to produce our positive results. By the final day, we all felt like family.

Samantha and I experienced many obstacles and emotions in the two weeks leading up to film week and the charity event, and with the support of our mentors and sponsors, we got through them. We all had experienced misunderstandings and arguments while preparing for everything. At one point in the middle of film week, we even thought that Shea was going to pull out of the show. As I mentioned before, sharing your story on camera can bring up anger and emotions. Also, when you put a group of type-A, high-achieving individuals in a room, initially it can be a struggle to get everyone to collaborate effectively. Everyone is used to doing things their own way and being the leader. We all learned to lead and follow at the right times. Even I learned to give others control of certain tasks and become the leader of that task. That wasn't easy for me, but it was necessary in order to pull off what we did.

We produced episode one of our show, pulled off a successful fund-raiser, and experienced a lot from the community. Now that we had accomplished the mission for our first city, we were already looking ahead to our next destination: Austin, Texas. It was a daunting feeling given we had no storyline or feature for Austin and didn't really have any connections there. Additionally, we didn't have any sponsors for the next episode.

While in Scottsdale, I had experienced some obstacles in my own business, Accelerant Media Group, which had been one of my main sources of income up to that point. I was buying out a business partner, and I had just had an event in Los Angeles two months before that set our company back. The event had experienced a major decrease in ticket sales due to fires that had been raging in the Los Angeles area. The event was supposed to have been the main revenue generator to set us up for 2018, but ultimately it became the event that set us up for debt payments moving into that year. This isn't something I shared publicly or with my peers at the time because I didn't want others to think I wasn't capable of pulling off our *Success in Your City* quest around the country. We had to keep many things secret. So many people thought that Samantha and I had it all figured out and were this successful couple filming our own TV show, but in reality, we were fighting to make ends meet so we could film it. We had many obstacles, and in our minds, we were far from being a success. We felt like we were living a lie at times, even though our hearts were in the right place to produce a successful show and help others along the way.

It became very clear that we were coming to the end of the road in funding, not only for our business Accelerant Media Group, but also for our personal finances. Our Scottsdale sponsors helped cover costs for the show, but we had to ultimately put in our own personal money to move ahead with film week there. We had used the last of our savings to create the Scottsdale episode.

Going into our mission with *Success in Your City*, from the start we knew we had completely underestimated how hard it would be and how much it would cost. This type of underestimating commonly occurs when people are trying to achieve big goals. With the next city upon us, all we knew to do was to travel to Austin and figure things out when we got there. There really wasn't any other choice, besides going back home, but in my mind that was never going to be an option. After the first week of February came and we had stayed at the mansion as long as we could, it was time for us to pack up our things and move on, even with little direction about where to go or what to do next. It wasn't easy to do, but Samantha and I had each other. We were on this mission together, and we were holding each other accountable to keep moving forward.

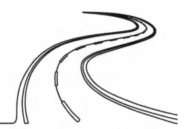

Chapter 2
Samantha Rossin in Scottsdale

Giving Your Time to Others

The moment we left our home for the year was bittersweet. Coming up with the idea to travel the country and redefine the meaning of success is one thing, but actually doing it was another. It was a cold December morning in Brandon's hometown in Iowa. We were rushing to get the Tahoe packed with everything we felt we would need for a year-long trip. Or should I say I packed our Tahoe? If I had let Brandon help, we probably wouldn't have survived longer than five days. Haha!

A rush of uncertainty overwhelmed me as I made countless trips in and out of the house. *Am I forgetting anything? Can we afford this dream of ours? Will people support us?* Soon, all of those questions would be answered but not without truly living what we set out to do. Besides, how challenging could traveling the country with my best friend be?

We wanted to make sure we got to Scottsdale before Brandon's birthday on December 31, so we split the twenty-four-hour drive into two days. Our drive was long but so beautiful. We traveled through the Colorado mountains and ended in the deserts of Arizona. It amazed me how we could be in one state one day and then easily drive to the next state the following day. Right before we arrived in the city, we got a message from our friend Robin, who confirmed that we would be able to stay in a listing that she had for sale in exchange for a marketing video of the property. We had been in contact with her since she had lived in Scottsdale, and she was so supportive of helping us in any way she could. She had no idea how much pressure released from my body when she called. Not many people drive through the entire country without having a game plan about where they will be staying. Brandon didn't need a schedule; he just went with the flow. Me, on the other hand, I needed to know exactly when, where, and why we were going to do anything. Low key, I wanted to get on Brandon's level of adventure, but I would never admit that to him. Haha!

Exhausted, we drove into Scottsdale late at night. I was so ready to arrive at our destination. The city was lit up so bright. I couldn't believe that in a matter of days we had gone from living in a town of seven hundred people to being in a city as big as Scottsdale. As we pulled up to a beautiful mansion, my eyes lit up. Although it was dark, I could see the outline of the home. It was so big. I mean like it could be in a movie big. Brandon jumped out of the car and punched in the code for the garage, and we pulled in. I laughed because the garage alone was the size of our house in Iowa. I had never been in a $3-million-dollar home. It was definitely on my list of what success should feel like. *This won't be so bad*, I thought. We unloaded our suitcases and officially started the beginning of *Success in Your City*.

The first night in the house was interesting. I was happy *and* scared. Since we had arrived at the house late, we didn't check the entire place out. The forensic side of me was visualizing someone coming out to kill us. I'm serious. I always played every scenario in my head, and the worst of all things was usually played the most. I don't know why I do it, but it drives Brandon crazy. So maybe that's why I do it? To get under his skin? Haha. As I was lying in bed, I was so anxious to get to the next day so that we could make this dream of ours a reality. A part of me was visualizing how this journey would go perfectly, and the other part of me was visualizing what a disaster it could be. We had told the world what we planned on doing, and I wanted to make sure that we lived up to it. The last thing I wanted was to fail and have everyone watch as we did. I needed to make sure that this journey was seamless so they wouldn't have room to knock me down with their words.

The next morning, we woke up and pinched ourselves as the view from the bedroom door was unreal. The sun was shining on the pool, and the mountains in the background made it a picture-perfect image. *Is this what success feels like?* I wondered. My definition of success was to be truly happy, but in the back of my mind I knew I wanted materialistic things to show that I had made it: a big house, a nice car, designer handbags. Those things filled my basket as well at this time.

We decided to get ready as we wanted to make the most out of the time we were in Arizona. I walked into a bedroom-size bathroom. The countertops were a beautiful marble, and the giant mirrors lined the entire room. As I turned on the shower all the way to hot, it stayed cold. Cold as ice. I waited a little longer, but I had a feeling that I was going to be taking a freezing-cold shower regardless. Immediately, I became upset. I hate being cold, and washing my hair in cold water would be a nightmare. I screamed at Brandon that there was no hot water and blamed him. How selfish of me, as he had no idea that we wouldn't have hot water. It was a house up for sale. Maybe they had turned off the hot water because it was on the market. I sucked it up and took a shower, but I don't think I've ever cussed more. *Why is this happening?*

As I got out of the shower, I was questioning my behavior as here I was in a beautiful home that we were allowed to stay in for free. How ridiculous to be complaining about something so little, I realized. It was clean water. I had shelter. Soon, this experience would make me grasp how thankful I should be for a warm shower that I have the privilege to have every single day. Every time I shower now, I think of that day and I appreciate it so much more. It was an easy fix as someone came to turn on the hot water. A huge lesson I learned: Be grateful for what you have because not everyone has the luxury of a warm shower.

Before the show planning started, we decided to find things to do around the city. The weather was beautiful, and coming from Iowa, where it can get to below zero, we wanted to take advantage of it. One of our mentors, Scott, gave us tickets to a college football game. This great gift made us feel welcomed. The game was fun, and it was a perfect way to start out our month in Scottsdale. Spending Brandon's birthday doing new things was another memory that I cherish. I knew I wanted to fill the day with exploring the city, so I woke him up super early on his birthday and took him hiking on Camelback Mountain. It was dark and cold when we started the hike. A couple of other hikers had backpacks and flashlights, and I soon realized that we were not prepared. I had just come up with the idea of the hike the night before, so I hadn't done much research. Oops. We started the climb anyway, using our cellphones as flashlights. The sun started to rise, painting the sky pink and orange. As we got to the top, I couldn't believe the view. I had no idea what we were climbing up to, and boy was it worth it! Standing at the top of the mountain with Brandon felt so freeing, and I was just so grateful to be "doing life" with him. I didn't actually tell him that though. I was terrible at letting him know how I felt, so instead I let him know in other ways, like planning things to do on his birthday. At the time, experiences were how I expressed my emotions to him.

Later that day, we decided to go to Old Town Scottsdale to see some shops and have dinner. I couldn't believe we were living in a city this beautiful. Looking around, endless possibilities confronted us: shops, music, food, coffee. Again, it was a pinch-me moment. *Wow, this is our reality.* After going into almost every shop, we ended up having sushi because yes, we are obsessed. We usually demolish like eight rolls together, and his birthday was no exception. During our meal, we had a long conversation about what we wanted to achieve and how far we had come. Brandon loves masterminding on his birthday about what we can accomplish. I used to find that super odd. Who wants to use that much brain power on their birthday? I will probably never understand, but over the years it's become something I love about him. The best thing about planning his birthday each year is that I actually plan things that I want to do. It's a win-win for me. Is that rude? Haha. He enjoys whatever I plan anyway, so if he's happy then I know it was a job well done.

We chose Scottsdale to be the first city to feature on our show after meeting Shea Hillenbrand and hearing his story in October 2017. Our mentor Scott had introduced us to Shea during a last-minute dinner meeting he set up for us. Unfortunately, I wasn't feeling good that night, so I stayed in the car and took a nap. We had just returned from a nearly thirty-day mini-road trip visiting some of the cities we wanted to feature, so I think exhaustion was kicking in. I felt bad that I had sent Brandon in to this dinner on his own, but I didn't feel my best. Maybe it played off me not feeling "ready" even before the journey began. I can't really tell you why because at the time I just felt sick. Brandon came out of the restaurant and shared with me what Shea had shared: Shea was a Major League Baseball player who had lost everything. I was intrigued. I wanted to hear more. Thankfully, I knew that I would be able to hear his entire story through our show.

Before meeting with Shea and the mentors, Brandon and I planned out what we envisioned. We wanted to positively impact the community as well as help Shea with his speaking. How would we do that? Shea and Scott mentioned the idea to raise money for the Boys and Girls Club. I had never been to a Boys and Girls Club, so I was interested in volunteering my time to help kids there. If there is one thing to know about me, it is my love for kids. It's always been important to me to make kids feel loved. They are such special gifts, and not all of them are treated with kindness.

Brandon and I had decided not to have kids, and I think we were put on this earth to help the kids who need us; the kids who are less fortunate to be born into a loving home. In fact, the more "unwanted" kids we meet, we feel it's a sign that we have been chosen to help them, to love them, and to listen to them. I knew I could help at the club, but helping Shea speak was way out of my comfort zone. I had never spoken in front of people, so I immediately felt like I wasn't going to fulfill my part as a cohost in this episode. Not only was that on my mind, but the thought of being on camera scared the crap out of me. Did I not think about that before I committed to filming the entire year? I guess not. And it didn't help that I was so stuck on how I was going to look or if I would look like I was acting. I didn't want to embarrass myself in front of other people as I valued the opinions of others—a little too much, if you ask me. In fact, the way I did things and the way I dressed had a lot to do with what others would think of me. In my head, I knew that what I would wear for a dinner meeting was based on what others would view me as and not necessarily what I actually wanted to wear. I had lived a lot of my life like this. It's so sad because so many of us hold back who we really want to be. For me, this tendency went back to the days of me trying to find my worth after being stuck in my addictions. I'll talk more about that in a later chapter.

When we met with Shea and our mentors for the first time, I was so nervous. They had invested in our dream, and I wanted to make sure they knew how much it meant. But instantly, I felt so detached at our show-planning meetings. As we sat at this big table in our big man-sion and brainstormed how to make the Boys and Girls Club event go smoothly, I couldn't help but think, why am I even here? I was over-thinking to the point that my stomach was in pain and I couldn't even get any words out. They were so successful and knowledgeable in their careers, and that intimidated me. I had nothing to offer compared to them. Constantly, I was comparing my accomplishments to their suc-cesses. I felt so out of place, which completely robbed me of my desire to help on the show. Their passion was so clear when they spoke. Why wasn't mine? I had trouble speaking the thoughts in my head. I always have. The stories and knowledge I have inside of me were there, yet it's the most challenging thing to get my words out in a conversation.

Quitting my job as a personal trainer had a lot to do with me feeling less important. I knew the show was going to take everything we had, but I felt jobless in a sense. So, as I was sitting with a group of people who had careers, I let myself strip away my own worth. I tore myself apart in the meanest ways, and there wasn't one thing that would change my mind. I felt so worthless. This was all coming from my own voice playing inside my head. None of them made me feel less worthy, it was all me. They were there to be a part of the vision of the show. They were putting their hearts into it. And I still was making up this story in my head that I didn't fit in.

I knew I was happy with who I was, but I let the story inside my head eat away at my worth. Literally, I made up what others could be thinking about me, and this led to me not giving my everything to the show like I had set out to do. Had I just remembered that everyone is blessed with different gifts, I could have had a different perspective on what was right in front of me. So many times, we compare ourselves to others to a point where we forget what we are truly capable of. I can't change how I felt about my self-worth at the time of the show meetings, but it left me with a very valuable lesson that remains with me: I may not have the same gifts as others and I probably never will, but I still have things that make me valuable. Accepting that and understanding my blessings have brought me another gift to add to my best self: the gift to not compare. Comparing myself to others was a one-sided fight with myself. It affected me and only me. Escaping those negative thoughts has helped me focus on what I can do and not on what I can't.

As film week was approaching, my entire body overflowed with painful doubt. I felt like I had no control over my emotions. But let's be serious, we all know that we control our thoughts. But darn, though, I was that girl who was drowning in her own puddle of "poor me." Not only did I feel out of place, now that the crew was flying in, I also realized that I did not understand what my part actually was. Brandon was helping Shea with everything, and I had no expertise in what he wanted. I felt defeated and pissed off. Why did I stop my entire life for this? Resentment toward Brandon was the only thing that filled my mind. All I could think was that he brought me into his dream and didn't consider how I would find happiness doing something that was so out of my comfort zone. It didn't help that people asked me multiple times if I was following my fiancé as he filmed his show. Those words cut into me deep. The last thing I wanted was to look like I was there to follow someone else's dream.

I had heart in this show too. Sure, I wasn't as "out there" as Brandon, but I wasn't about to change who I was for the show. I always envisioned myself as being more behind the scenes. Deep inside, I knew that I was a huge part of the show, but it sucked knowing that people were thinking exactly what I thought they would. It sucked because I was struggling with finding who I was, and now I had everyone else wondering who I was as well. I seriously had to question myself: *Who am I?* I couldn't even answer that question. Brandon didn't understand why I was hurting. Continually, he assured me that I would make an impact, but I was not seeing it.

All I could think about was how everyone saw this as Brandon's dream. They thought I was just along for the ride. This made me feel unfulfilled. I wanted to quit. I had no intentions of this happening, but my heart wasn't in it. I literally felt like I was the wife of a professional football player and all eyes were on him as I stood on the sidelines being pushed out of every conversation because I wasn't who people wanted to hear from. I couldn't see how I could make an impact. Even though I was the biggest cheerleader of our lives together, it seemed that I didn't matter. I hated my thoughts. I hated that I was spending so much time comparing myself to others. I didn't think the month would put me in a place of not knowing my role. All my excitement turned into me being miserable and exhausted in a matter of weeks. On top of my negative thoughts, we were struggling to fund the show. The worry of money always intensifies tension. We had so much to pay for and being short on money gave me another thing to worry about. We not only had the show to pay for, but we had a mortgage back home on top of a car payment and bills. How were we going to make everything work?

With all my emotions on the table, I was looking forward to going to the Boys and Girls Club of Metro Phoenix. I met with John, who runs that location, and he showed me around. All the rooms were full of kids. They were playing games, coloring, playing at the park, doing homework, and even playing basketball in the gym. They had created a space for kids to come and not only feel safe but to learn and play. I felt so lucky to hang out with them. They were so funny, and although they didn't let me win any of the games we played, I enjoyed every second with them. I could see the hurt in some of the kids and as we played, they slowly put smiles on their faces. It felt good to give them my time. I didn't know what was going on with them—maybe they were bullied or maybe they had some things going on at home—but if I could make any kind of difference by giving them my time, then I was happy to be there.

It was hard to not become attached to the kids. As they shared stories about what they loved and what they didn't love, I realized something huge about time: Time is the thing that they valued most. They didn't ask for gifts or money. They just wanted you to listen to them, to interact with what they wanted to share. These kids awed me. I've never looked at giving back as simply giving kids my time. It's always been associated with money or materialistic things. These kids I had never met before gave me the gift of knowledge that day: the resource of time and what it does for others. We can never get time back, and that day made me realize that I need to spend it wisely on the things that matter—on things that fulfill me, not on what everyone else is doing. It made me realize that I was going to live the best life I could. I went into that club thinking that I was going to teach the kids something with no idea of the value I would get in return. Those kids are a blessing to me and to anyone who will listen to and learn from them.

I left the club wanting to do more. What kind of experience could I give them to make their constant daily struggles go away? I wanted them to shift their mindsets, even if only for the time that I was with them. Fitness was the one thing that I used to fuel my future to become the best version of myself. Movement of any kind is proven to make us feel better. I asked John if I could take the kids through a workout, and I was happy when he said yes. I asked the guys from FunkFit fitness, who we had met a week before, and they agreed to lead the workout with me. While in the gym, all the kids were so excited. I've never seen so much energy in one room. All their focus was on what we were about to do. We lined all the kids up and had them do warm-up exercises. They listened, laughed, and asked questions the entire time. For that hour of movement, they were definitely living in the now. Nothing else mattered to them. There was no negative energy in that room. All the positive vibes were shining through their entire bodies.

As the class ended, I sat down on a bleacher. The kids had experienced so much more than a workout class. We had all come together to forget about all of our worries. My way of thinking changed after spending time with those kids. I didn't need to pretend to be someone I wasn't for them. I didn't need to bring them gifts. They valued the time that we shared. All they wanted was to show us what they were talented at or to share a story with us that they loved talking about. Meeting those kids changed how I viewed time, and I'm grateful for spending it with them because they helped me put a new perspective on giving back. I got to live in the moment with them and remember what life is all about.

Hearing Shea's story about his identity had got me thinking about who I was. Why was I doing the show? Who was I doing it for? These were powerful questions, and I wasn't proud of the answers. Almost everything revolved around making other people happy; making other people think I had my life together. They didn't see my pain from not feeling involved in the episode. I always put my happy face on and did what I felt I needed to do. The month in Scottsdale was hard. It challenged me more than I ever thought it would. I struggled with who I was and what my part of the show would be. I realized that everything I was doing revolved around others' opinions. Sometimes it was all made up in my head. Letting my fear control the experiences that we had made my time less enjoyable. I had put way too many stories inside my head, and for what? As much as I learned from our experiences in Scottsdale, especially from the kids at the club, Shea's story opened up a lot of questions about who I was. I was hoping that throughout the journey I could answer those questions in a way that truly made me happy. Not momentarily happy. Truly happy.

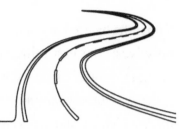

Chapter 3
Brandon in Austin

Faith, Love, and Never Giving Up

Friday, February 9, was the day we left the mansion in Scottsdale and drove toward Austin. We didn't know where we would be staying there or our exact plan, but we knew that being in that city would help us clarify our plans. Samantha and I made our road trips fun (at least from my perspective). We listened to music and a lot of audio books. Napoleon Hill's books always seemed to inspire and motivate us, especially when we had no energy to give. On our long road trips, we always made it a priority to make a pit stop to work out at a gym. Working out relieved a lot of stress and gave us time to forget about all our problems and obstacles. It was our time to better ourselves physically and mentally.

After driving all day, we hit up a random hotel somewhere in Texas. Our hotel stays on the road really made me feel like we were gypsies. We would travel through all these random towns and meet so many people. When they asked what we did for a living, I always proudly said that we were traveling the country and filming a TV show together.

Samantha hated that attention because she hated how we had to explain ourselves. The first thing people would say was, "What network is it going to be on?" Since we were still filming the show and weren't doing it the way others would, we had no idea what network would pick it up. We always said we were planning on being on NBC, ABC, Netflix, or Hulu. Upon hearing those words, it was frustrating to see the doubt in others' eyes. Since we didn't have a network deal already, everyone just thought we were working on a "project" that might go on YouTube or somewhere. I don't know why it bothered me so much, but I hated it when people called our show a project. It made me think of a school project or something amateurish. No one knew the sacrifices we were making to produce this show and do this trip. People didn't take us seriously right away, and that is what drove me to keep pushing harder. I knew we were going to prove others wrong one day.

The next day, we started day two of driving to reach our final destination, Austin. That day, we had set up a dinner meeting with a married couple who have a real estate business in the city and were potential candidates that we would feature on episode two of our show. Their names are Ricky and KodiKay Cain. Mandi Monaghan, one of our sponsors and mentors on the Scottsdale episode, referred them to us.

As soon as we got into Austin, we booked a hotel for four nights since we didn't know where we would actually be staying or for how long. Since we were Club Carlson members, we got a rate of $79 per night with the points that we had. We unloaded our stuff into the hotel room and got ready for dinner. We needed to make sure we made a great first impression on the couple we were meeting, because if they were a great fit for our show, we wanted to make them feel comfortable enough to allow us to share their story on our show.

Samantha and I hit it off right away with Ricky and KodiKay Cain. They were positive people and a powerhouse couple that had come far together. Over dinner and drinks, we got to know one another better and asked many questions about their own journeys. After an hour into the dinner, Samantha and I knew that they would be the couple we would feature on our next episode. They had an amazing story, and we knew that many viewers would relate to it. They also had a nonprofit called Cain Cares that they had recently created. Its focus is to renovate homes in need in the Austin area. For every home they sell, they take a percentage of the profits and put it toward Cain Cares. After dinner was over, they told us to come in on Monday to meet their real estate team to become acquainted with everyone.

That night, Samantha and I brainstormed ideas about filming with the couple and how we could collaborate with them in Austin. We had already decided that we were going to feature them as our success story, but we hadn't gotten a commitment from them yet to appear on the show. We knew we had to demonstrate the value of appearing on it.

Monday morning, we showed up at the Cains' office bright and early. We met all of the team members and witnessed KodiKay practice sales scripts with each of their agents. KodiKay taught the team how to deal with objections; she also taught them the best phone tactics to get people to commit to an in-person meeting to discuss listing their home. It was quite impressive to see how well their team worked together and the commitment they had to being the best real estate team in the city of Austin and eventually the state of Texas. I personally had sold real estate in 2012 through 2014 and had learned the ins and outs of the business, but the Cain team's tactics were foreign to me. There was a reason they were among the top ten real estate teams in Austin. Another thing that stood out: The team members weren't just coworkers or employees of Ricky and KodiKay's—they were like family. They prayed together before starting their day and attended church together. If they weren't working together in the office, they were spending time together outside the office doing fun activities. They really encompassed the meaning of what a team should look like in a business.

After meeting with the Cain team and talking with the Cains further, the couple agreed to help us create the second episode of the show and be its featured guests. They also were going to work with us and their network to find sponsors to fund the next episode. The only issue was that they were going to be out of town for the next week attending Keller Williams Family Reunion. They made it clear to us that they wouldn't be able to help out much over the next few weeks, but we were fine with that. We didn't really have an option at that point. What Ricky and KodiKay didn't know was that we were down to our last dollars and had no place to stay yet. We weren't as lucky as we had been in Scottsdale, where we'd had someone willing to allow us to stay in their mansion for six weeks in return for a promotional video. Something that we also didn't account for was the South by Southwest festival (SXSW) in March. That jacked up all the rates for hotels and temporary units during our time in Austin. Samantha and I knew we were about to experience some obstacles in the road.

The next two weeks became the hardest of our lives together and put our relationship and mission to the test. We ran out of money completely and were living on credit cards. My bank account was negative a few thousand dollars because I had automatic payments coming off for business expenses that occurred monthly. Every single day over two weeks, I had to update my banker to let them know that I was close to having some deals coming in and just needed some more time. My other business, Accelerant Media Group, was short on cash as well because we had just made the final payment to buy out a business partner. They say when it rains, it pours, and during this time it felt like the perfect storm was raining down on us. Luckily, we had some free nights at our hotel and could charge more nights on our last credit card. This is no joke; we were eating Ramen noodles and hot dogs every day and ate the free cookies at the hotel's front desk.

I tried my hardest to stay strong and keep a positive attitude even though we were in a very bad situation. Samantha cried every day and begged me to get her a plane ticket home. I told her that we just had to keep going. Part of me felt like I was a bad fiancé to put us in this situation, but part of me also told myself that it would give us a better future, and I really believed that. In the meantime, Samantha became really depressed and our conversations together were at a minimum. We sat inside that hotel room wondering what we were going to do. I felt like I was going crazy, like nothing was going to work. I sent emails, did coffee meetings, posted videos online to drive awareness, and kept looking for sponsors to get us back on our feet and to focus on the development of our show's mission. The memories of that hotel room will stay with us forever.

I would email Samantha and write her notes time to time to let her know how much I loved her. Sometimes that was the only way to get the message to her because we weren't really speaking. Valentine's Day came, and I wanted to give Samantha the world but there wasn't much I had left to give. I had a few hundred dollars of credit on my credit card and I took her on a date and dinner for Valentine's night. Yes, I was spending what little money we had left, but I wasn't going to let the woman I loved sit in a depressing hotel room and eat Ramen noodles on Valentine's Day. That night we weren't fighting, and for the first time in a while we had our own romantic moment together and I was reminded of what mattered most to me in life. Samantha was my success. She was the woman I loved. She was the woman who believed in me and walked beside me in pursuit of achieving the craziest of dreams. I wasn't about to let her down. Failure was not an option.

Lessons Learned from Being Broke and in Love

When you are in love with someone, but you don't have much to give financially, I believe it's your duty to show that person how you feel in different ways other than buying them jewelry or fancy gifts. Some of the best gifts that I have given to Samantha are handwritten notes, emails, gym dates, and an occasional dinner date (this woman loves food). Be resourceful and use the things you have to create something special for your loved one. It's the little things that count. Don't ever take your significant other for granted, and always let them know how much you appreciate them. As humans, we always want something fresh and new, and many people think the grass is greener on the other side; but I've learned to realize that when you appreciate what you have and show gratitude toward that person every morning and night, you will love them even more.

Finding Faith and God

When times are tough, most people start praying. Samantha and I were no exception. We prayed more than we had ever prayed in our lives. The Cains had told us about their church, Riverbend, and how their senior pastor Dave Haney gave a very powerful message that speaks right to your soul.

We attended Riverbend Church the following Sunday together by ourselves. We felt like we were supposed to hit rock bottom for a reason—because if we weren't at rock bottom, I don't think we would have turned to God or attended Riverbend again. Dave's messages were powerful and uplifting. We looked forward to attending Riverbend and felt empowered every time we were there. As we grew closer to God, Samantha and I grew even closer to each other. Our relationship became stronger, and our current situation didn't bother us as much. We started to believe it all was happening for a reason.

February was our struggle month, but March came and we began to see progress. God started to answer our prayers. Ricky and KodiKay's real estate business became a sponsor of the show, and they also helped us recruit other sponsors in their network who had a strong business relationship with them. I also had been working on a consulting deal for six months, and it finally came to fruition, so thankfully, I was paid a pretty large sum of money. This allowed Samantha and I to leave the hotel and move into a furnished apartment on a thirty-day lease. We finally had a place to cook meals and be motivated. Funny enough, the apartment was literally right across the highway from the hotel we had lived in for a month.

Now that we had funding again, we started to go full throttle on planning the scenes for the next episode and creating the storyline. We did countless calls with Shawn Vela, our director, and Jonathan Hickey, our script writer. While setting up all this filming, we were also planning a fundraiser with Ricky and KodiKay for their nonprofit, Cain Cares. We planned to bring in speakers for the event and use ticket sale proceeds and donations to pay for the renovation of a home for an elderly couple who lived a few blocks from the Cains. The homeowners were Melba and Marvin, the nicest couple that you could ever meet. They more than deserved to receive the gift of a home renovation, and we were determined to help them in a big way.

How to Be a Team in Business and in Your Relationship

We spent a lot of time with the Cains and their entire team to prepare for the Cain Cares fundraiser and to find the right locations to film. In March, we became like family with the Cains. We learned so much from them about business, family, and how to have a relationship that works. Ricky and KodiKay had built a business together that they had started from nothing. A relationship takes work, but when you have a business together as well, that ratchets up the difficulties. Samantha and I knew this from our own experiences as entrepreneurs, but we hadn't put in the amount of time on the entrepreneur-couple front that the Cains had.

At a one-on-one dinner with Ricky one night, he told me to always date my wife. He said that it's vital to always go on dates and to never take things for granted. Sadly, many couples stop dating and stop being romantic with each other over time. This is the quickest way to lose your connection with someone. Since our time in Austin, Samantha and I make it a priority to go on at least one date per week, even if that means staying in, cooking food together, and drinking wine—preferably $2 Buck Chucks—while watching Netflix. The point is to spend that quality time together.

The relationship tips the Cains shared with us also related to business and having a powerful team to win with in business. Their team went out together on team dates, like bowling, eating out, and playing Wii at their home. As I mentioned previously, they went to church together and prayed together. Everyone supported each other as if they were family. I really believe that to have a successful team of any kind, you must become like family. The days of having a boss who bosses you around are over, at least for the millennial generation. Instead of being the boss, you can be the leader who coaches your team to greatness. Ricky and KodiKay made it clear to everyone on their team and others interviewing to join the team that their mission was to help them achieve any goal they set their minds to. They also made it clear that they would be there to hold them accountable and coach them along the way. Their success was also the Cains' success.

Just like the Cain team, our entire team for *Success in Your City* was like family. We accomplished goals together as a production team that no other production team would even think about achieving when filming a TV show. We had many dinners together that were unforgettable. In every city, we found Airbnbs to cram into to save costs and to film testimonial scenes for the show. Everyone on our team witnessed fights between Samantha and me, and they saw us shed many tears in the process of filming. Each one of us was also committed to creating the best show while also making each other better. At times, I had very high expectations of the crew and made them film as late as one a.m. to get the shot we needed; and they did it because they knew it was necessary. They did it because they believed in the vision. They believed in the vision Samantha and I had, which ultimately became all of our visions together. This was about more than producing a show; it was about creating a movement around changing the way people view success.

Film Week in Austin

Wednesday, April 4, was day one of filming for episode two of *Success in Your City*. We had 3.5 days to film eleven scenes that were spread around Austin. Some scenes included a date night in a coffee shop, a fundraiser event (that we needed to actually put on), driving around with Ricky, eating bacon donuts at Gourdough's, having dinner with the Cains, playing Monopoly, collaborating with the Cain team at their office, renovating Melba and Marvin's home for Cain Cares, and more. Not only did we have to film the show in 3.5 days, we also needed to put on a fundraiser and transform a home in twenty-four hours. Let's just say that my nerves started to kick in after thinking about everything we had to pull off.

Many memorable moments occurred during the filming of this episode, but the scene I will never forget is the romantic dinner at the coffee shop with Samantha. We rented out Johnny Beans coffee shop for the night, and put rose petals and candles all over the place and on one table at the center. We set it up to look like a romantic candlelit dinner scene.

Samantha and I had dinner together in the middle of that coffee shop, and I surprised her with a note I had written. As I read it, we both cried.

I read aloud:

Samantha,

This has been an interesting start to our year. Many ups and downs. Things haven't gone as planned, but we always made it through and came out on the top.

We are unstoppable together. Without you there is no show, there is no journey, there is no success. From Garnavillo, Iowa, to Scottsdale, Arizona, to Austin, Texas, and who knows where next. As long as I'm with you, it is a success.

Success to me is being able to spend the rest of my life with you and enjoy this crazy ride together.

You are my success. And I love you!

As our tears flowed, I realized that this was one of the realest moments on set that we had experienced together. Yes, there may have been six people around us filming the scene, but we didn't notice them. We were focused on each other. We had just overcome the biggest obstacles over the past few months, and we had done it together. We reflected on our journey while eating the dinner in front of us, and we got to have our date night while being filmed for the show. It truly was remarkable. It's moments like these in life that you live for. It's the little things that you never forget. This scene became the most romantic scene of the entire season, and it was totally unexpected. Sometimes in life the best things happen to you when you least expect them and when they do happen, be sure to enjoy the moment and don't take it for granted.

The next day was the fundraiser for Cain Cares. I had called in my friend James Whittaker to be a featured keynote speaker to help us sell tickets. James wrote *Think and Grow Rich: The Legacy*, which went along with the movie we had produced together. We also had the sponsors of the Austin episode speak on their areas of expertise. This was a perk that came with being a show sponsor. We provided each sponsor their own video and gave them the opportunity to speak on their own topic of choice. Only about 50 percent of the attendees we thought would show up were there, but we were determined to make do with what we had. The event didn't raise the money we had hoped for, but it spread awareness of the Cain Cares mission. It also allowed us to recruit about a dozen more people to donate their time to renovate Melba and Marvin's home. Sometimes someone's resources and time can be just as powerful or even more powerful than any money they could have provided.

Friday, we renovated the home. As many as thirty people were there at one time helping out. We painted walls, put in new flooring, landscaped outside, put in a new fence, put on new roof shingles, and decluttered. Our film crew captured it all. Samantha and I felt like Chip and Joanna Gaines as we acted like we knew what we were doing to fix up the house. I felt proud that I had put in new flooring for an entire bedroom, something I had never done in my life. We had started working on the house at six a.m. and stopped for the day around nine p.m. It was pretty cool to see what we had accomplished in such a short period of time.

The next day, we finished up the final touches on the house and made it feel like a new home. Working on the house and spending time with Melba and Marvin fulfilled us more than anything we had done while in Austin. I believe they gave more to us than we gave to them. When you do good for others, it makes you feel good about yourself.

Lessons Learned in Austin

Ricky and KodiKay Cain gave us more than they will ever know. Our experience with them taught us valuable things about our relationship, team building, and the power of giving back.

Relationships. You must always date your wife or husband! Always keep your romantic side alive and never take each other for granted. Before Samantha and I got married, the Cains told us to write expectation letters to each other. In these letters, we would state our expectations about marriage, such as the idea that we should always push each other to become better, always go on at least one date night per week, always let the other person know when something bothered them, and so on. Writing such a letter is a must for anyone looking to get married! Make sure you do it before you tie the knot, and if you are already married, write your letters now if you haven't already.

Team Building. Treat your team like family. Help your coworkers grow and achieve their goals, and together you will go far. Everyone must hold one another accountable. Outside of work, engage in important activities that aren't work related. Build a real relationship with your team, and they will fight with you all the way to the top.

Giving Back. The Cains advise that you use your resources to show that you care. For every home that they sell, they put a percentage of the profits toward their nonprofit to renovate homes in their community. Beyond money, you can use your time and resources to show you care by giving back. The more that you do for others, the more fulfilled you will be.

Samantha and I gained faith while in Austin—faith in each other, faith in God, and faith that we could overcome any obstacle together.

We attended Riverbend Church one last time before leaving the city. That Sunday, the first words that came out of Dave Haney's mouth blew us away. These unexpected words jolted Samantha and me into instant belief in, and dedication to, our mission. These words solidified what we were doing. I believe God was speaking to us that day.

This is what Dave said:

"What is success?"

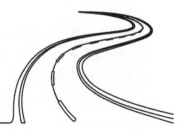

Chapter 4
Samantha in Austin

The Power of Choice

As we drove toward Austin, I was hoping for a fresh start. Not because of the people or experiences in Scottsdale but because of how I felt. I was not looking forward to another long month of feeling out of place. On top of that, on our road trip into Texas, Brandon and I began doubting that twelve cities in twelve months was going to happen. We had to revamp our plan. We talked about hitting just six cities.

This talk about changing plans put me in a negative frame of mind. We would not be reaching our original goal. *Will people look at that as a failure?* I asked myself. *People will focus on what we didn't do and not on what we did do.* So many thoughts danced in my head. Here I was again caring way too much about what others were going to say. We were happy with our decision, yet I still felt anxious about the changes for *our* dream. Ridiculous. But how many times do we stop doing something or feel bad about something in exchange for what other people think? All the time. No matter how much we tell ourselves that others' opinions don't matter, the negative thoughts still creep up in our minds.

I still believed in the vision, but I definitely didn't share Brandon's elevated level of passion for the show. And soon, we were about to experience hitting rock bottom.

When we arrived in Austin, we went straight to dinner to meet KodiKay and Ricky for the first time. I was pretty cranky as we had just driven ten hours, but part of this journey was meeting new people. I was excited, but do you ever plan something and then become so irritated and tired from life? That was me. Regardless, I always show up and am always so happy I did.

KodiKay and Ricky met us at one of their favorite restaurants. We had previously talked to them on the phone with an introduction from Mandi, one of our mentors and good friends. Thank you, Mandi! As we ordered drinks, I couldn't help but appreciate the way they communicated. They said everything with so much gratitude. Their energy was unbelievable. KodiKay appreciated every detail that the waitress was offering, and you could see how that made the waitress happy. KodiKay was so genuine, and she instantly inspired me to slow down and appreciate the exact situation I was in. How powerful to gain something so important from someone you just met. We talked a lot about life and how energy attracts energy. She and her husband also told us about their nonprofit, Cain Cares, which we wanted to raise money for. It impressed me then, and it impresses me now, that KodiKay and Ricky take a percentage of each sale from their real estate business to renovate the homes of families in need. That's just incredible.

That Monday, we had plans to meet the Cains for a tour of their office and to be introduced to members of their team—not something I was looking forward to. The thought of meeting new people makes me nervous. Sometimes my heart races, and I feel like I'm going to puke. No matter what I tell myself beforehand, it doesn't help. I might be able to tell myself I'll be okay, but then right when I meet someone, all of that disappears and I'm back to my heart-racing self.

Brandon and I pulled up to the building under the bright, shining sun. It was a beautiful day. We walked in the door like we knew where we needed to go. Actually, we didn't, and that just made my stomach hurt worse. My God. Talk about not being able to control your emotions. Brandon messaged the Cains to let them know we had arrived, and soon, someone from their team met us in the front.

Quickly, we were led to the elevator and up to the Cains' office. Inside, positive words and awards hailing their achievements overflowed. KodiKay introduced us to the team and described how they start each day. Very quickly, it became evident that this team was like a family. Immediately, I felt so comfortable with them. They accepted Brandon and me into their office, and for that time I felt like we had no worries. We brainstormed with a team member named Grace about how we could put on an event to raise money for their nonprofit. I was hoping I could be of help in this area as the business side of things wasn't my expertise. I always left that part up to Brandon.

Later that day, we drove to our hotel and discussed everything we needed to do: Find a place to stay. Find scenes for filming. Book flights and an Airbnb for our team. It doesn't seem like a lot, but it was time consuming. Finally, after we got settled, we scrolled through Airbnbs, furnished apartments, and even corporate apartments and realized a very limited number of places to rent were available. Not to mention they were super high priced. As we asked around, we discovered that finding a place to stay would be the worst of our problems. Having it so easy in Arizona, we thought that we'd just land a resting spot in Austin. So wrong. We learned that South by Southwest was going on and that a majority of Airbnbs were taken. We wound up in a Country Inn and Suites using points and cash. It wasn't good enough for me;

I wanted to feel comfortable and "at home." And Brandon had promised that we would always find a place that would feel like home. Our stay at the hotel turned into a month. Thirty days of misery! And that is an understatement. What we experienced during those thirty days literally tore us apart; I had my bags packed and was ready to leave. Without Brandon.

I had no idea that staying in a small hotel room for an entire month could put so much stress on us. When we left Scottsdale, I had envisioned everything going a specific way and this was not it. Shame on me for trying to force an outcome. Complaining about staying in a hotel room now seems ridiculous because it's a "luxury" problem to have. But back then when we were living it, I was so mad at Brandon. We were low on money, which was a huge reason why we couldn't afford some of the apartments that were left for rent. Actually, no, we weren't low on money; we were out of money. All of the money coming in was going to the show. Literally every single penny.

Brandon was putting the show above everything else. This made me question how he would take care of things when we were actually married. I built up so much resentment toward him, and he never understood why. We were scraping by to pay for the hotel room, and there were days we didn't even eat. Like, did he remember who he was dating? I love food! Brandon seemed okay with everything and continued to work toward the show while I lay in bed feeling helpless. They say you're never ready, but when we had to starve ourselves to fund the show, that crossed the line.

Brandon would have slept in the car, so what did he care. He would go buy hot dogs and Ramen noodles, and I seriously looked at him like, "Who are you?" Prioritizing the show over us was not his best moment and as his soon-to-be-wife, I became angry. Angry to the point that I didn't talk to him for days at a time. If he asked anything, I would just nod, expecting him to figure out if it was a yes or no. How selfish of me. I hated our situation, and I blamed every single ounce of it on Brandon. He had made us start this journey before we were ready. He had dragged me along on HIS dream. I believe I forced myself into a deep depression. I held everything inside of me and was silent for weeks.

At a time that my fiancé needed me, I failed him. I ignored him and blamed him for things out of our control. I threw a self-pity party thinking that would make things less painful. So, there I sat in the hotel room with no words and no want to help him succeed in OUR dream. I felt so defeated. Why would we choose to go on this journey unprepared in hopes to INSPIRE others? It just didn't make sense to me. I needed a sign to know that we would overcome this obstacle.

As the weeks passed, sadness overwhelmed me. I was weak from limited food. That, coupled with our lack of money, made me think we'd have to give up the show. I wanted to give up. I wanted so badly to leave and never look back. But Brandon didn't let that happen as he was always the one who picked up the pieces of my brokenness and helped me get my life back together. But this time, as I was at my lowest, something so unexpected happened. At what seemed like the perfect time, KodiKay and Ricky introduced us to their church, Riverbend.

At first, I had no interest in the church. I was stuck in this terrible place, depressed, feeling so alone. The last thing I was going to do was go find my faith. I was in such a negative place, and my stubbornness always took over. I hadn't been to church in years and never found myself thinking about faith. The night before, on a Saturday night, we were feeling lost. Sitting in the hotel room, it was dark and unwelcoming. We were so sick of trying, trying to find a place, trying to stay positive, trying to assure each other everything was going to be fine. We had a conversation about giving the church service a try. We'd hardly ever talked about faith in the five years we had dated.

That following Sunday, we drove to Riverbend. I felt anxious. In the past, I had been to church, but I never felt the message related to me. I was hoping this service would be different than what I had experienced because I really needed something to tell me I was going to be fine. When we got to the doors, everyone was so welcoming and asked if we had any questions. Never had I experienced something like that before. Inside, I was surprised to see a band standing on the stage. The room was so big and beautiful. Instantly, I was so intrigued by what was about to happen. The band started to play music. The words were up on the big screen, and everyone sang. The band impressed me. Their love flowed from the words they sang, and the energy in the room was full of love. You could literally feel it. Brandon and I stood up and started to sing. We rocked back and forth to the beat and for the rest of the time, all my worries disappeared. I was in the moment, oblivious to time passing.

The senior pastor came out. His name is Dave. He started to talk about his family and that he was happy everyone was there. What he said next got my attention: "Thank you for choosing to be here. I know all of you are here for different reasons." He then went on and said, "Some of you are forced to be here with your parents, and some of you just needed to be here. You're here because the darkness and the difficulties of life are wearing you down and you needed to get somewhere to find some hope." I was in tears. He was speaking right to us. We were there because we needed to be encouraged that we would make it through our filming journey. He continued on to pray for his family and for everyone at the service. I had never felt so connected to someone I had never met. All I could think about was that I wasn't alone. Even in this big city that we had never been to, I wasn't alone. I could go into this church and find a community that accepted everyone and anyone and didn't judge us for what we were going through. I was in awe.

Pastor Dave spoke deeply to us about choices and that maybe the answer we have to wrestle with has to do with having the ability to choose. Immediately, I thought about the choices I had been making. I was choosing to hurt Brandon by ignoring him, and I was choosing to only focus on what we didn't have. Pastor Dave ended with a deep message I still hold close to my heart: "God chose to love us. We are loved by God even when we don't realize it." He went on, "Make the choice, regardless of the darkness, to choose love. The choice is ours." At the end of the service, I was so emotional. I kept these feelings inside because I was still a little resentful toward Brandon, but I felt something come over me.

Brandon and I went back to the hotel, and I lay in bed thinking about how I could make the most out of what I had right in front of me. This whole journey was me fighting with the negative thoughts in my head. I didn't see the good in any of what we were experiencing. I wanted to change that. I wanted so badly to get back to the place where I was excited about exploring people's lives. I wanted to go back and live the visions I once had for creating this show. I wanted to have conversations with my fiancé. We were barely talking, and if we did, it was through texts or emails, even when we were in the same room. We hadn't even explored the city together like we had in Scottsdale, and it was all because of me. I couldn't help but think about what the pastor shared with us. We had been led there for a reason. It was such a defining moment for me to realize that I needed to change my perspective on the situation that I was dealing with. I needed to understand that to move forward, I had to press into what was right in front of me. I might not see the good in everything, but there is always something good to take out of the experiences we deal with.

I looked around our dark hotel room, our home for the past couple of weeks, and I started to cry. I felt so suffocated and terrified by the idea of staying another night. I just wanted to feel like I had a home again. I kept questioning why I couldn't see the good in the situation. The fact that we had shelter, a place to brush our teeth, and a warm bed to sleep in were all good things. It literally hit me midcry that the good things in life don't mean luxury items. They don't mean that for me to be grateful I need what the person I look up to has. Having the good things in life is about being okay with what is right in front of me.

As I pondered the meaning of what constitutes a good life, I realized that I could continue to be upset or I could take what we did have and continue what we set out to do. I cried for a long time that night. I wasn't sure if I was happy or sad, but I understood one thing: We have obstacles right in front of us that can be negative and positive . . . and we have the choice to choose how we react to them. We have a choice to be grateful for what we have or to be resentful about what we don't have. I decided that I was going to choose gratitude. Thankfulness for the car we were driving, for the warm hotel we were staying in, for the clean water we were drinking, and for the opportunity to make friends with members of the Cain team. Everything started to become so clear to me. My life was fine. The problem was my mindset—something that I could change. I was going to think differently from now on, and I had the church to thank for that.

The following day, I wanted to talk to Brandon about everything. I had been so focused on him not giving me the materialistic things that he had promised, which I equated to him not giving me all of his love; *"He didn't give me a comfortable place to stay, so he must not love me." "He couldn't feed me the nutritious food that I wanted, so he must not love me."* These negative thoughts had prevented me from seeing what was right in front of me. Brandon was still taking care of me. He was dealing with my pain because he loves me that much. He did everything he could for me with the situation we were in. He loved me through his emails, through going out and trying to find us a place to live, through putting his accounts into the red for us to live our dream. He had been loving me all of this time, and now I was finally able to see it. I was finally able to put my hateful thoughts aside and appreciate what he was doing for me. What he was doing for us.

I expressed to Brandon how sorry I was as we sat in a Starbucks trying to find a short-term apartment to lease. I broke down. I didn't want him to feel like he was doing this alone, and I know that was on his mind. I had been so caught up in what we didn't have that I didn't support him with anything that needed to be done. He told me that he understood why I was so down and that he just wanted to see me happy again. He said he was sorry. We just sat there and prayed to find the strength to move on and not look back.

It took another week for us to find a place. Ironically, it was right across the street from our hotel. When I realized that I thought, *Are you flipping kidding me?* But that's exactly how some things work. As we entered the apartment, happiness overwhelmed me. The apartment had a big living room with a couch that we could relax on. It had a kitchen that I could cook meals in again. Like REAL food. A bedroom where I could hang our clothes. And somehow my favorite thing was the washer and dryer. I guess not having a washer and dryer for a month really makes you grateful when you do have one. I think I spent the first couple of days just doing laundry, happily. We took the next week to explore the city and find things we wanted to highlight. Our business partner Mike flew in to stay with us, and together we got everything we needed to prepare for film week.

The week finally arrived, and the film crew had just landed so we headed to their Airbnb to talk about the week ahead. I always liked to fill their fridge with drinks and snacks so that they didn't get too hungry. If I weren't there, Brandon would "forget" to feed them. He can go hours without eating, so sometimes his consideration for feeding the crew was, well, not there. We would have so many things to do in a short couple of days, and we needed our fuel! No one wants to be around hangry boys. Shawn, Carlos, Jeff, and Kai had become family to us while in Scottsdale. They had already experienced my emotional side, my happy side, and my angry side, and they still wanted to be a part of the journey, bless their hearts. But really, I had become so open with these guys, and I was so grateful that they chose to continue to help us create the show. During the week with them, we did a lot of stuff in a little time, but my favorite memory was always going back to the Airbnb and talking about what we accomplished and what we could get better at.

All the crew members had insight about different things, and I learned so much from them—like how my emotional side was important to help even out Brandon's business brain. I had always found my emotional side to be a negative aspect of me, but I was learning that life is hard and it's okay to express emotion in different situations. It's also important to express it and move on. Just like energy, it affects the people around you, so the last thing I wanted was to be that girl who whines about every little thing—even though I was feeling like I was that girl on this entire journey.

The crew also made me realize that we were doing hard stuff. Not many people can pack up their car and go live a dream with limited resources in each city. They always reminded me that failure is okay and that just like my past I could use it to become a better me. I seriously give these guys so much credit as I was superdifficult to deal with, and I would literally cry all the time. They just continued to believe in what we were doing and to be supportive regardless of my mood.

My favorite experience during film week was renovating an elderly couple's home. The Cains had chosen the lucky man and woman whose house we were going to renovate with the funds from Cain Cares. I was honored to contribute a helping hand to this project. Melba and Marvin, the chosen couple, had been married for decades and had brought up all of their children in their home. Their place was on a corner lot that needed some outdoor work. We were also going to remodel a couple of bedrooms and declutter the kitchen to create more space for them to enjoy their time together.

Renovating the house with the Cain team, our crew, and all the volunteers was so much fun. The volunteers showed up bright and early and KodiKay, with her big heart, brought in coffee and breakfast burritos to help everyone get fueled up before the work began. I admired her for so many reasons. She was so clear about her intentions for the day and focused so much on how she could help others. Watching her inspired me to start being more grateful for what I did have and not focus all of my energy on what I didn't have. Girl, I wish I'd met you sooner in my life! Some things are out of our control, and we spend so much time focusing on what we want to happen, the way we want it to happen, that we don't leave space for things to happen the way they are supposed to. This leads to a lot of disappointment. From watching KodiKay, I learned that if I let negative energy control me then that is all I will get in return. Energy attracts energy no matter what kind. KodiKay came into my life at a time when I needed her. I needed guidance from someone who I could look up to. I thank God it was her. She was so easy to talk to and was so open to helping me learn something I needed so badly in life.

Positive thoughts and actions reward us. We must practice sending out positive thoughts and feelings every day and in return, we will receive positive outcomes back. We may not see it right away, but that's because sometimes we go back to our habits and the things that make us angry so easily, which results in bad energy. That was me—the entire month. I focused all of my time on what we didn't have, on how "bad" my life was. In return, my life suffered from negative things: a stressful relationship with Brandon, no opportunity to make money, limited food. I never thought I would be someone who would look at life this way, but when you truly live it and start to see it change from the simple fact of being positive and grateful, it's life-altering. It takes time. And sometimes the positive things that come back to us are small, so we tend to look past them; but when you can appreciate even the smallest things, your perspective changes. Everything you think and say becomes your reality. So, think about what you are filling your head with every day. Are you living a life of intent? Are you finding gratitude? If not, think about how you could change the direction of your thoughts. What could you replace those negative demons with so that you can experience what KodiKay gifted me? Surround yourself with people who inspire you and lift you up, and you will start to see changes in the way you think and live.

Melba was standing at the door as we finished eating. She had a huge smile. She was such a beautiful lady. She had her hair pinned back on each side and was beaming with so much positive energy. I just wanted to hug her! Which I did! We went through the garage, which was stacked with boxes of stuff that she and her husband, Marvin, had accumulated over the years. As we got inside, we were introduced to Marvin, who was in a wheelchair. He was a little quieter than Melba, but we soon heard many stories about the woodwork that his dad created, which was all over the house. He also told us stories about his days in World War II.

Meanwhile, we all worked so hard to complete our projects in the short time frame we had, and we succeeded at that. It's amazing what you can get done with a hard-working team who loves to give back. The house renovation completed our time in Austin. We said our goodbyes to the Cain team and headed back to our apartment to get ready to head to the next city.

As I look back, the way I acted with Brandon breaks my heart. Yes, it was painful. And yes, I had become angry about the fact that we didn't have money to eat some days. But we were experiencing life in a way that we had dreamed of that day in Puerto Rico. Brandon had never promised me a smooth sail. He had never said that every single situation was going to be handed to us. I knew how trying times were going to be because I had watched him fulfill his entrepreneurial lifestyle for the last couple of years, and I knew how tough *that* had been. It's hard to go after something much bigger than ourselves. It's even harder to stand up after getting knocked down as hard as we did. At that time, I couldn't see the strength in the situation. That's because I didn't give myself the opportunity to do that. The negative energy that I created that month was a CHOICE. I had no want to even think positive because I hated what we were experiencing.

Now, when I think of our time in Austin, I see so much more than pain. I see growth. I now know that we could have had it way worse. We could have been sleeping in our car with no access to a clean shower. We could have quit and gone home. We could have broken up. Yes, I say that because I was in a place of resentment and anger. At the time, I blamed it on the person I loved most. Life could have been so much more painful. If I had just shifted my energy to what we did have and what we could do, I know that we could have made more progress. That's hard to admit. I had no faith to reach out to at that time. It wasn't until we started to go to church that my thoughts slowly started to shift. The pastor spoke so deeply to me and ultimately to us to let us know that everything was going to be okay. I'm forever grateful for Ricky and KodiKay leading us to that church because it saved our relationship, our dream of pursuing the show, and my perspective on every situation we were put in.

They say God only gives you what you can handle, and as much as I fought that during that month, I now can look back and appreciate the lessons learned.

Chapter 5
Brandon

Accepting Change and Learning to Let Go

We left Texas as a totally new couple. We had conquered many obstacles, our love was stronger than ever, and we had faith again. And now, we had no idea where we were going to drive to next. In March, we had made plans for our next stop to be Kansas City, Kansas, but some of the things we had planned to do there had fallen through. The connections we had in the city did not have the time required to help us feature Kansas City on the next episode of the show. It didn't bother us because we knew that everything would happen the way it was supposed to happen. As we had already found out on our tour, things weren't going to go as planned and we were going to have to adapt to change along the way. We knew that we had to be in Des Moines for my event the Young Entrepreneur Convention from April 19 through 21, but our next stops were undetermined before that time.

While approaching the Texas border, we put Nashville, Tennessee, into our MapQuest. We knew that it was going to be one of the cities on our tour, but we didn't know exactly when yet. Besides, we were planning to have our wedding there in October, and we still needed to book a venue for our reception and ceremony. Samantha was starting to get stressed out with the wedding being only six months away. I'm going to be the first to admit that I was not much help with it. *Success in Your City* consumed my mind, and Samantha's was consumed with our wedding experience, just like any woman's would be. Nashville always had a special place in our hearts because it was the first city that Samantha and I experienced together in 2013 when we first started dating.

Over the next few days in Nashville, we checked out venues that might be a right fit for our wedding. We wanted to wed on October 13, 2018, exactly one year after we got engaged. Soon, it became clear that many venues in Nashville were booking one to two years out. That started to worry me because I wanted to make sure that Samantha would experience the wedding of her dreams at the location of her dreams. When we thought there was no other hope in finding a Nashville venue, we looked at one more space, The Bell Tower. It's a renovated church that is one of the oldest churches in the city.

As we walked up to it, Samantha gave me a look that expressed her dislike of the place, but as we walked in the door her expression started to change. She really liked the inside setup and how beautiful it looked. She could envision herself getting married there. Personally, I was good with whatever made her happy as long as they would allow us to film the wedding for our TV show. It turned out that a corporate event had had the venue booked for October 13 but had recently canceled, leaving the date open for us. It seemed almost like it was meant to be. Within twenty-four hours, we booked the venue and locked in the dates. There was no looking back! Our venue contract was signed, and our deposit was paid. We officially were going to get married in Nashville on October 13, 2018.

Friday, April 13, we left the city and drove ten hours back to my hometown, Garnavillo, Iowa. One hundred seven days had passed since we had been there. We decided to spend the weekend in our home there before heading to Des Moines for my event. Over the weekend, we went through all the stuff that we had brought with us on the trip and started to eliminate the things we didn't need during our travels. Many of it was unnecessary clothing and cooking utensils. It turns out that it's much easier to rent furnished units while traveling the country, which eliminates the need for utensils, coffee pots, towels, cleaning supplies, and many other things that people use every day. As we went through things that we didn't need for our trip, we noticed that we didn't need hardly any of it! We started packing garbage bags full of clothing and other things to donate to Goodwill. Getting rid of things that no longer added value to our lives was freeing.

How often do you keep things that you no longer need? Is it that favorite T-shirt or pair of jeans you loved in high school but haven't worn in years? Time to throw them away or give them away! Is it that extra set of cups you have from a random party or event? Time to throw away or give away! Is it those school papers you have stacked up from high school or college? Time to burn them! What about those old photos of you and your ex in a shoebox? Yep, burn that too!

More isn't always better. When it comes to "stuff," less is better. Less stuff means fewer things to think about and more valuable things to focus on. This is the main reason I wear the same black shirt and black pair of jeans from Express every single day. I have fifteen black T-shirts and eight pairs of black jeans to choose from. Not having to think about what I'm going to wear allows me to save my brain power for focusing on my goals and more productive things. This simple lifestyle change has made me happier, and it has also made it much easier for me to pack my bag for travel.

Over the weekend, Samantha and I decluttered our house, cleaned it, and questioned why we needed to own it any longer. I built the house in

2012 after graduating from college and since I moved in, I was always traveling and never there more than seven days at a time. It was just another payment that automatically came off my bank account each month. We talked about selling the house but weren't quite committed to letting it go yet.

That Monday, we drove to Des Moines, about four hours from Garnavillo. We had many friends in Des Moines because we had moved there in 2014 to start a company together. That company ultimately failed but it led us to meet many people in the city and it led me to cofound the Young Entrepreneur Convention. It was also the city where Samantha got into personal training and group training classes. Many memories were made there, and many of our favorite restaurants, such as Fong's Pizza, Wasabi Tao, and Scenic Route are there. We both are big foodies and dinner dates happened often in Des Moines.

Throughout the week, I attended meetups, saw old friends, went to 1 Million Cups, and appeared on a local morning show to promote our event. Many of my entrepreneur friends from all over the country flew in to attend the event. The Young Entrepreneur Convention had become known throughout the country as one of Iowa's largest entrepreneurial events since it started two years before and was even recognized nationally and internationally. This was the event that allowed me to build up my brand and influence in the entrepreneurial community. It also was the event where I had Kevin Harrington and Jeff Hoffman speak at during our first ever event in 2016. That was the first step in building a relationship with them, which eventually led to them executive producing *Success in Your City*. It is easy to say that the Young Entrepreneur Convention built the initial foundation and connections necessary for Samantha and me to pursue our vision to travel the country and film the TV show around success.

During the two-day event, I connected with many entrepreneur friends in Des Moines but also close entrepreneur friends who had flown in to support the convention. This year's event was different than others. My passion for it remained, but I was more focused on *Success in Your City* and hadn't put into the convention the heart and soul I had in previous years. It still had an amazing turnout, and we had many recognized speakers for our lineup. That Saturday night after the event ended, one of my cofounders and I went to dinner with our pitch finalists and our featured keynote speaker, Jason Calacanis. During four hours at dinner, we talked and Jason gave us targeted feedback. If you don't know Jason, I highly suggest you check out his book *Angel*, which gives you great advice if you want to become an angel investor or to get investors for your business.

During dinner, Jason told me a few things that helped me gain clarity about decisions I needed to make next in my entrepreneurial journey. He also told me that I needed to focus on my goals and on what I really wanted to do in the coming years. He told me I was working on too many things. He also said that I should start an investment fund to put money into other entrepreneurs like the ones sitting at the table with us. His feedback was on point and credible, coming from one of the top five angel investors of all time who is known for turning a $100,000 investment into $100 million. As I drove Jason back to his hotel that night, his additional feedback made it clear that I needed to change some steps I was taking on my entrepreneurial path . . . and that this wasn't going to be easy.

Soon after the event took place, we scheduled a team call to go over the future of the Young Entrepreneur Convention. That call ended with the idea of me stepping down from the event full time and becoming an advisor moving forward. My cofounders and I felt like it was the best decision for the success of the event. It was going to be necessary if I wanted to make *Success in Your City* the major success I had dreamed of. Our success tour and show needed all of my focus in order for us to achieve our goals. The Young Entrepreneur Convention was originally my idea in 2015. It was a part of my identity, and I was proud of what it had grown into. Walking away from the business full time was very difficult, a decision that took me some time to make. Samantha had helped me fully realize that it was the right thing for me to do, and she held me accountable in following through with my decision. If she hadn't, I would have kept working with the company, not being able to give it my full attention and energy, which also would have resulted in less focus on *Success in Your City*. By June, I officially sold the majority of my shares and stepped down from the Young Entrepreneur Convention full time, becoming an advisor.

Lessons Learned from Letting Go of Things and Selling a Business

It's hard to let go of things that have been a part of our lives for a while, but if we don't, we will never allow bigger and better things to come into our lives. Sometimes we need to let go of material things that no longer do us justice in having. At points in our lives, we may need to let go of significant others or relationships that no longer make us better or support our vision. There are also times when entrepreneurs will have to decide whether to let go of a business or endeavor to succeed in another. It was difficult to let go of my control and authority in the Young Entrepreneur Convention and to step away from something that I had cocreated, but if I hadn't, you would not be reading this book today and *Success in Your City* would not be in the position it is today. After shifting almost my sole focus to the show, a weight was lifted from me and I felt more focused and driven to succeed. I had one less thing to worry about.

When one door closes, another one opens. What doors do you need to close to open the doors that you have been wanting to walk through your entire life? Change isn't easy, and most people are resistant to it, especially when things are good. But good isn't great. Great things happen out of your comfort zone and while pursuing the unknown. My heart wasn't 100 percent into the Young Entrepreneur Convention anymore, but it was 100 percent committed to the success of *Success in Your City*. If you want to see something reach its fullest potential and succeed, you will need to focus on it 100 percent. Yes, you can run multiple businesses and give each the most attention possible, but you won't be able to give either one the 100 percent focus necessary. You will be able to find success, but you won't be able to reach your full potential for success. This was always something I knew, but it wasn't something I was able to commit to as an entrepreneur.

After I let go of the Young Entrepreneur Convention, I still owned Adams' Ice Service, but there were very few daily duties there that I needed to manage. My dad was doing that for me, but the time was also about to come when I would either sell the business or find someone else to run it. It was just a matter of time before I was going to have to confront that situation, which I had been dreading for a while. Change is good, but it is hard. The only way to open one door is to close another, and the only way to reach the fullest success in something is to put your sole focus on that ONE thing. That ONE thing for me was *Success in Your City*.

Back on the Road

Now that the event week was over for the Young Entrepreneur Convention, we had no other obligations in Iowa, and nothing was holding us back from traveling to our next city on the tour. The only thing was, we didn't know exactly what city we would be going to next. While in Iowa, I had a deep conversation with David France, who was at the event for the week. David is a good friend of mine who has always supported my entrepreneurial endeavors. He helped me find funding for the TV show *Ambitious Adventures*, and he was also one of the first supporters of the Young Entrepreneur Convention in 2015.

David is one of the most interesting guys in the world, and when I say that, I really mean it. You just never know what to expect from him or who you may see him hanging out with. One day you may find him couch surfing around the country attending events, the next you may see him meeting with the CEO of some Fortune 500 company. David is a minimalist who doesn't have a lot of money nor does he want to spend a lot of money, but if you put a monetary value on his business connections, he would be a multimillionaire. He was living in Boston and has a youth orchestra that he created from the ground up. He literally was homeless in the process of building it. His story always amazed me and continued to amaze me as I learned more about him, and it had crossed my mind a few times to feature him on our show.

After the event, Samantha and I spent a week in our home in Garnavillo to devise our strategy on what to do next. Finally, we decided to travel to Boston to feature David's story on the show and to figure out how to fund the episode after we got there. Sunday, April 29, we made our way toward Boston. We made a pit stop in Cleveland, Ohio, to meet with our executive producer Jeff Hoffman. We sat down with Jeff at the original pancake house the next morning, Monday, April 30. As we ate breakfast, we talked about the progress of the show, about what we should do next to ensure that we find the funding necessary for the next episode, and about what tactics we should use to approach networks to pick up our show. Jeff always had great advice and shared stories of his experiences landing major sponsors for other projects he had been a part of. Jeff always answered our questions with a story from an experience and gave us a takeaway at the end of the story. He's by far one of the best storytellers I have ever heard.

I will never forget when Jeff told me that success is having your loved ones with you to share it with. He said that me having Samantha by my side on this journey is what success really is. He told me that no money in the world could ever buy what Samantha and I had. I believed him, and I still believe what he said to this day. It was fascinating to hear that from a man who had achieved so much success in business and making money. Jeff has had more experiences than anyone I know. He has flown around the world and worked with presidents, princes, celebrities, and world leaders. He has even spoke at the United Nations multiple times.

After a three-hour breakfast meeting, Samantha and I said our good-byes and were motivated again to make Boston, what we had determined would be the next city on our tour, a huge success! We had no idea where we were going to live and how we would fund the next episode, but we were going to figure it out. We had less than a month to do it because our film crew was already set to film with us in three weeks. It was the only film date available besides mid-June, and we didn't have time to wait around that long before filming episode three. We needed to stay on track for filming season one, and we also needed to cut costs for living in the city.

Chapter 6
Brandon in Boston

Networking Like Pros and
Meeting Boston Ballers

We arrived in Boston late on Monday, April 30, and spent the night in a hotel. The next day, we already had meetings lined up with influential people in the city that David had introduced us to by email. We were focused on meeting as many people as possible right away and sharing with them our vision of the TV show. At the end of the meeting, we would ask for an introduction to anyone they might know who might have an interest in being featured in a scene or becoming a sponsor of the Boston episode. It's difficult asking for sponsorship money from someone you just met, and it's even more difficult getting someone to commit with only a three-week filming notice. The things we had going for us were that David was well respected in Boston and we also believed in our mission more than anything in the world. When you believe in your mission and the product you are selling, it will be much easier to sell it.

After a few meetings, we sat in our parked Tahoe in some random neighborhood and started calling up furnished apartments we found online that did temporary leases. We weren't about to make the same mistake we had made in Austin and spend a month in a hotel. The thing we didn't account for was that May was graduation month, meaning all hotel, Airbnb, and corporate apartment prices were jacked up for the month. We called up many places, only to find out they were booked or were way overpriced. We finally found a place to look at that was in our price range. The next day, we toured the apartment and we were sold on the place. They told us that it was available to move into right away; we agreed to move in that next day. Four hours after leaving the apartment showing, the leasing agent called to say that they had made a mistake and the apartment wouldn't be available for another week! Talk about superfrustrating, and we felt like we were in the same position we had been in in Austin. After getting that call, we were determined to find our apartment within the next twenty-four hours. We weren't about to spend a month in another hotel.

We found a place downtown that was the smallest apartment I had ever seen and was directly above a subway station. It was way over our budget and a half-mile walk to where we had to park our vehicle. Time wasn't on our side, and we couldn't waste any more time looking for places, so we booked the apartment. It was the most money we had ever spent on rent, and it still hurts thinking about it, but we had no other choice. Time is money, and we only had so much time to raise funds for the next episode. We decided on the place so fast that it wasn't until after moving in that we realized the unit didn't have a washer and dryer. Samantha wasn't too fond of that, but we made it work. The good news: We had a place to live during our time there, and it wasn't a hotel. Now, it was time to focus on meeting people, finding places to film, and locking down some sponsors.

Networking Like Pros

I think Samantha and I set a record while in Boston for doing the most coffee meetings in person in such a short period of time. David gave us this idea to create a podcast series called *The Boston Ballers*, where we would interview all the people we met up with and publish them on my existing *Live to Grind* podcast show. This was a way to add more value to the people we met by promoting them to our audience. This also made it a cool experience for the person we met, meaning they were likely to remember us and become more likely to help us with the show. We made the interviews short and to the point, lasting around ten minutes each. They took place in a coffee shop or in the interviewee's office and focused on success and what success meant to the guests. Each person mentioned something around their desire to give back and help others.

Spending time with family and friends was also a common theme around the meaning of success. Each interviewee inspired us and gave us more passion and drive toward creating the show and helping people in the city. If you want to listen to the *Boston Ballers* podcast series, the episodes are 350 to 357 on the *Live to Grind* podcast show. We interviewed local celebrities, social media influencers, violinists, owners of coworking spaces, individuals who helped in the elections of past presidents, and people who were creating a better future for Boston.

Besides coffee meetings, every Thursday I would attend the Venture Café networking event, which turned out to be the best place to find connections. Samantha stayed back because networking events aren't her favorite thing. She also got tired of us having to explain ourselves and our *Success in Your City* journey. Not many people understood us, and many continued to think that this was just some fun project we were doing, even though it had become our life. The first Thursday I attended the Venture Café event, I grabbed an open mic and spoke in front of 150 people for two minutes about our show and what we were doing in the city. After speaking, many people came up to me, which gave me an opportunity to share our mission in more depth and find potential leads for show sponsors. Besides finding leads, I was also asking others what they knew about David France and how they had met him. Many people knew David because he had been attending the Venture Café event for years. Hearing stories about him from other people gave me more ideas about how to best tell his story on camera and capture the best content for the show. The more I knew about David, the better we could go deep into his story.

Every Thursday after attending Venture Café, David and I would grab wings at his favorite restaurant. We talked about the show and different ideas around where we could shoot scenes for his episode. Every time, meeting with him was a mastermind session. David is a wise human being and one of the smartest guys I know. He looks at things differently and is always thinking outside the box, which helped us during the process of planning the shoot with him. After spending more time with David, his motives in life and what makes him happy became clear. We found out what success meant to him and how he was achieving it.

David loves to help others and give them the insight, connections, and guidance to achieve their own goals. This truly makes him happy and is what he looks forward to. He always put others before himself. His famous quote is, "Giving your life away for the joy of others." Anytime David meets someone, he wants to find out as much as possible about that person so he can help them through his vast network of influential people. He has built up this network because he always comes from a place of serving and providing value, instead of wanting something from others. Many people have the "what's in it for me" mentality, which is why they are less likely to connect with other people of influence. When you meet a person for the first time and go into the conversation from a place of serving and adding value, they are going to be more likely to remember you and stay connected with you, especially when you deliver massive value to them over time. This is exactly how David has been able to connect with billionaires, CEOs, celebrities, and some of the most influential people in the world. People of influence are always being asked for help in some form or another. If you flip the script and be the person who offers to help them, this will ultimately allow you to build a connection with them over time.

There is a valuable lesson to take away here that everyone should be applying if they want to get closer to their goals and connect with anyone they desire: Be like David and add value first in any relationship. Don't expect anything in return. Use your resources, knowledge, and connections to help others get closer to their goals. The more people that you help and the more value that you give, the more value you will get in return over time. As the late motivational speaker Zig Ziglar said, "You will get all you want in life if you help enough other people get what they want."

The more time we spent with David and everyone he had introduced us to, the more we wanted to give our lives away for the joy of others. Our meetings led us to form relationships and become friends with these people. Then it started to bother us that we had to find sponsorship money for the show. Everyone wanted to help, but it was such a short notice before filming. Our hearts believed in the show and mission more than anything, and we believed in the value we were providing with our sponsorship levels, but we also believed in the add-value-first approach. We didn't want to go straight to "Hey can you sponsor our show?" after only knowing someone for less than a month. After two weeks, it became clear to us that we would not be getting any sponsors for the Boston episode.

Before arriving in Boston, Samantha told me that if we didn't find the sponsorship money to film the next episode, she wasn't going to be on board with us filming. She didn't want us to spend any more of our own money on the show, and she didn't want to end up like we had in Austin: broke and negative in the bank account. We had some money available from my past consulting deals, but that was our only source of income at the time. I hadn't been pursuing clients for a while since my entire focus was on the show. After going back and forth, we committed to spending what was left of our own money to fly in our crew and film the next episode, featuring David's story. Samantha had anger toward me for spending our own money, but I understood where that emotion was coming from: We had a wedding to pay for in five months. I kept telling her that it was an investment in our future. I always told her that it all would pay off one day. I always knew it would, I just didn't know when or how many more obstacles we would have to overcome before it did. Everything always takes longer than expected and is way harder to achieve than you plan.

Chapter 7
Brandon

Giving Your Life Away for the Joy of Others

The David France Story

David was the son of immigrants who moved to the United States from Nevis, a small island in the West Indies, to pursue the American Dream and provide a better future for their kids. David started playing the violin at seven years old while facing a society that told him that violin was not an instrument for black people. He overcame that bias by putting in more than 10,000 hours of practice by way of playing with teachers, at free events, festivals, and locations around the world. In 2011, he won a fellowship that allowed him to travel to Venezuela to join a training program. While there, a woman named Isandra Campos, a mother of five, inspired him. Isandra had moved out of her home and moved in with her mother so that the neighborhood children could use her home to play music every day. Seven days a week, children would go into her home to sing and play various instruments.

Isandra raised chickens in her backyard and sold their eggs, investing the money back into the music for the kids. Her sacrifice gave them a chance at a better life. The ability to play music provided them a platform that would allow them to go further in life and achieve their own success. Their success was her own. She enjoyed seeing these kids succeed; she was devoted to them.

Witnessing what Isandra had done for these kids made David realize he no longer had any excuses for his mission to start a similar orchestra. After a few months in Venezuela, he returned to Boston and ended up falling in love with the community of Roxbury. He was determined to create a world-class orchestra for the youths there. After graduating from the New England Conservatory, David subleased his apartment and spent the next six months sleeping on couches and on the streets of Boston while devoting his time building relationships that would help him create the Roxbury Youth Orchestra. Nothing was going to stop David from creating this orchestra. He spent many nights sleeping outside behind the Boston Aquarium. He had meetings with billionaires during the day to get valuable advice, and he spent the cold nights sleeping on concrete. He knew that if Isandra could achieve her dream, he could achieve his too!

In February 2013, the Roxbury Youth Orchestra was launched in the auditorium of Dearborn Middle School. Just six weeks later, NBC News heard about what David was doing and sent a crew over to film his story. The famous Chelsea Clinton covered it. That story led to David sharing his experiences at a national conference. Over time, he went on to become a keynote speaker around the country and to even give a TEDx Talk. During his journey in creating the orchestra, David has also had the honor of performing with John Legend, Smokey Robinson, and Quincy Jones, and being the concertmaster of the first YouTube Symphony at Carnegie Hall.

Roxbury Youth Orchestra is a safe house for youths in Roxbury. It gives them a place to play—and create—music together. David says an orchestra is a model community where members must listen to each other and work together to achieve success. The goal is not to just give the kids a place to go but to show them how to make a home. David is striving to create a lasting community upon a tradition of equity, opportunity, and confidence that comes from music. Through the orchestra, he believes he can affect executive function skills and teach twenty-first-century workforce skills. David wants his students to walk away feeling empowered to walk onto the streets of Boston armed with self-esteem and the will to dream.

David has been named among the top 100 most influential people of color in Boston and a Top 40 Urban Innovator Under 40 in the United States. He has also written the book *Show Up! Unlocking the Power of Relational Networking*. His book shows you how to connect with anyone and how to build real relationships in business and in life.

What I Learned from David's Story

David's story always reminds me that where there's a will there's a way. You can either figure out how to achieve something, or you can make an excuse about why you didn't achieve it. David went to the extremes of sleeping on the streets of Boston so he could continue to pursue his mission of creating Roxbury Youth Orchestra. Most people would have thrown in the towel and moved in back home with their parents. How many times do we make up excuses for why we can't achieve something? What excuses have you been making that have been limiting your success or holding you back from reaching the goals you have set? I've always said that you will either figure out a way to achieve something or you will make an excuse about why you couldn't achieve it. From time to time, I catch myself saying "I can't" or coming up with an excuse about why I can't do something, then I think of David's story. This pushes me to figure out a way to overcome the obstacle that lies ahead of me. Anything is possible if you just keep going. All successes come at a price. The question is, are you willing to pay the price?

Meeting the Roxbury Youth Orchestra

Samantha and I took the subway from our place to Roxbury to meet with David and his orchestra that we had heard so much about. When we arrived at the school, we were greeted by one of the students at the entrance, who took us up a flight of stairs and into a hallway that led to a cafeteria where David and his students were playing a song. David welcomed us in and introduced Samantha and me to the class. Over the next few hours, we watched as David taught his students and worked with each of them to perfect their skills and harmony playing. Most of the kids were teenagers, but one kid was four years old. He was there with his mother watching the group play and holding up the fake instrument that was used to teach him the proper way to hold a violin.

David was a strict teacher who pushed his students to achieve excellence. As they worked together to play a song, you could see the bond between all of them as if they were family. For some of the students, this was their only family. Similar to our experience at the Boys and Girls Club in Arizona, most of these kids didn't have the best place to go home to. The Roxbury Youth Orchestra was their home and the place where they could learn the fundamentals of life. Their success in the orchestra would flow into their lives and future success. We left the class that day inspired and motivated to share the Roxbury Youth Orchestra with the world. David, the kids, and anyone involved with the program deserved the spotlight.

The Filming Begins

The film crew landed in Boston the night of Monday, May 21, and we were filming right away on Tuesday morning. We had our scenes and shoot locations picked out and had just received approval to film testimonials in the Airbnb we had rented for the week. We had four days to capture all the content for the episode, and there were eight scenes to film. This was fewer scenes than the Austin episode, but the obstacle in Boston was getting around the city from scene to scene. Boston isn't the easiest city to move around when you have equipment and cameras. We had to do a lot of moving on foot and using the subway system. Some of the scenes in this episode included visiting the orchestra, going to the Venture Café for a networking event and a meetup at Harvard Square, David busking at the subway station, and David putting on a Baller dinner. Each scene was a vital part to telling David's story in the most effective way. We also captured some scenes with Samantha and me planning our wedding and shooting some engagement photos.

Baller Dinner

Many memorable moments occurred during filming in Boston, such as David playing violin where the Boston Massacre took place, him playing at the subway station, and me learning how to play violin. You can witness all of these moments when you watch our TV series, but the most impactful moment I want to share with you now occurred at the Baller dinner. This dinner is something that David does occasionally, where he invites influential people from the city (Boston Ballers) to have dinner together. He doesn't just invite them to dinner, but he requests that everyone bring a certain ingredient for the meal. When you arrive to the event, there is no dinner ready because each item that people bring in is used to make the dinner. Everyone who is invited must work together to prepare and cook the meal. While doing so, everyone talks and builds a relationship and bond. It's quite enjoyable and refreshing. It gives you an entirely new look at a dinner meeting or networking event. After the dinner is ready, everyone eats while talking about stories in business and life and journeys around the world. David brings in the best of the best for these meals.

Prior to filming the Baller dinner, David had invited us to one so we could experience it firsthand. At that dinner, Samantha and I had the privilege of meeting a few other award-winning violinists who had been through David's orchestra program. One of them was Kiyoshi Hayashi, who is among the top 1 percent of violinists in the world and also a personal trainer. Kiyoshi shared how David's program had impacted him and taught him many life fundamentals. Hearing from people like Kiyoshi about David's powerful impact made me feel more fullfilled that we were going to be sharing David's story with the world. Since that dinner at David's house, I have kept in contact with Kiyoshi, and since then I've coached him in building his brand as a musician and trainer. He has also, along with a guy named Josh Knowles, played at one of our mastermind events in Miami, Florida. Josh has also participated in David's program and even appears in the orchestra scene of our show. I share this with you to show you the power of connections and relationships, the power of Baller dinners like David's. David's network has become my network, and now Kiyoshi and Josh are my good friends and business associates. When you SHOW UP to dinners like David's, you will be rewarded in ways that you can't even imagine. This includes attaining new friendships, lifelong friends, new clients, business associates, and a wealth of knowledge.

We filmed the Baller dinner at an Airbnb our film crew was staying in. David invited some friends and another violinist, Danny Koo, over. Danny is quite famous in the music world and has his own TV show, *Pinkfong*, similar to *Sesame Street*, airing in another country. We prepared pizza for the Baller dinner. It was fun prepping the meal and having conversations. The film crew was filming the entire experience but from time to time, they jumped into the conversation and enjoyed it with us. We were all becoming one big family. Preparing a meal together and eating together is a tradition that humans have participated in since the beginning of time. When you think about it, dinners or eating any kind of meal is a big part of our lives—business dinners or lunch meetings, dinner dates with your loved ones, birthday dinners, wedding dinners, and so on. Everything revolves around food and eating together. Having dinner with someone or a group is one of the best ways to bond. David figured this out and made it into a regular thing with his Baller dinners.

The pizza was out of this world! While cooking, we may have smoked the place up a little bit and even set the fire alarms off (that's on camera and wasn't planned) but the food turned out great. After dinner, we sat in a circle and told stories. David shared how his parents came to America to pursue the American Dream, and he shared his background as a child. Danny had brought his violin that he named Postiglione and played a few songs for us. He blew us all away when he told us his violin was worth $250,000! I couldn't believe it! I had never known how much these kinds of instruments cost. He didn't have to buy it, and it wasn't exactly his property; an organization had provided it as a form of sponsoring him. He has the rights to take care of it and play it over the next ten years or so. This opened my eyes to the ways of the music world and what being a violinist may be like. As Danny played, we all listened and lived in the moment. It felt like there were no cameras around us. It was just us and Danny playing music. You could see the pure passion on his face as he played the violin. If you ever watch a seasoned violinist play you will notice the pure passion and love they have for their music. It's like they are one with their instrument. Having passion for what you do is vital, and it will show in your work.

Being a Fiancé and a Cohost

We wrapped up the Baller dinner scene around midnight and said our goodbyes to everyone who attended. It had been a long day of filming, but a memorable one. Samantha, I, and Griffin Bruehl, a friend who was helping us film the Boston episode, drove back to our apartment so we could get some rest for the next day of filming. Our biggest day of filming lay ahead, and we only had five or six hours to sleep before having to get up and do it all over again. As we drove back to the room that night, Samantha and I got into an argument around how packed the filming schedule was. She was exhausted and hated that she had so many scenes she had to be in. It also didn't help that there were no other women on the team. She didn't have another woman to talk with during filming or a makeup artist to make sure she looked how she wanted to look on camera. Our filming budget was so tight that we couldn't justify having a makeup artist with us on set. She also hated that she had to wear so many different outfits in one day. She isn't like me, who just wears black clothes every day. All of these little things that bothered her built up over time and every once in a while, she would blow up over something. I didn't blame her for that, but I also knew that we just had to deal with things. That night, she told me that this was the last episode she was going to film. She wanted to be done with the show.

I was Samantha's fiancé, but I was also her cohost and business partner. When we had fights like this about the show, I had to balance how I handled the situation as a business partner/fiancé. As a business partner, I wanted to push her, and I did. I wanted to motivate her and try to convince her to do the things necessary to make our show a success; to make our mission a success. I also knew that everything we were doing would help her and her career as well. As a fiancé, I wanted to sympathize with her and make things right so she would be happy in the current moment. I didn't want to make her do anything she didn't want to do, but I also knew that by doing all of this for the show, she would become a better person and overcome her own fears and negative beliefs she had built up in her head. Samantha still had things from her past that needed to be tackled, and I felt that slowly sharing it all on camera would be the therapeutic sessions she would need to eventually overcome it all. I truly believe sharing your story on film is a powerful thing that can help you overcome your past and become more comfortable sharing your story with the world. When we share our stories with others, it inspires them and also empowers us all in the process.

I'm sure you can imagine how difficult it was being a fiancé and business partner at the same time. I always loved Samantha more than anything and always wanted the best for her, but sometimes what I believed to be the best for her, she didn't believe was the best for her. I was committed to her success and her personal growth. I was also committed to us creating the best show possible. Looking back on the experiences filming, I will admit I probably seemed like a selfish fiancé who was making his soon-to-be-wife do whatever was necessary just for the success of the show. I was committed to pushing Samantha out of her comfort zone and into the woman she was born to be. While in the midst of these times of frustration and the argument between us on film week, I always told myself that in the end it all would be worth it. In the end, Samantha would thank me for pushing her. The only fear I had was this: What if Samantha couldn't handle it and left me? These are the thoughts that came to me time to time, and I had to deal with them myself.

Lessons Learned in Boston

Friday, May 25, was our final day of filming. It was also the last time we would be seeing David during our stay in Boston because our apartment lease was up on Monday and we had to make the nineteen-hour drive back to Iowa. During our time with David, we had committed to listing our house on the market and accepted an offer while in Boston. We officially were going to be homeless and have no choice but to move on with our success tour around the country.

In the last scene of the Boston episode, we met David in the middle of a bridge over a river. We said our goodbyes and thanked him for the experiences and new relationships he gave us while in the city. We also gave David our very first wedding invitation, and we asked him if he would play the violin as we walked up the aisle. He was honored and said yes! Our Boston experience had come to an end, and we had gained another perspective on life and success. This was the third city that we had lived in within five months. In each city, we'd had unique experiences, made connections, and learned lessons. Each city made us stronger and prepared us for another adventure ahead.

David had provided us with many experiences and connections in Boston, more than we could have ever expected. We may have not had any sponsorship money to film the Boston episode, but our connections and experiences there were worth way more than any sponsorship dollars we could have received. Our investment in the Boston episode gave us more than our money's worth. As always, David had overdelivered and provided massive value to us. While living in Boston, we learned three main lessons from David.

1. **Be Resourceful.** You can do a lot with a little, as David told us. You don't need a lot of things to find success. You don't need a lot of material things or even a lot of money. David created the Roxbury Youth Orchestra from nothing. He had instruments donated, teachers donate their time, and even had his teaching location donated. Even when David was homeless, sleeping on the streets, he still kept going and figured

out ways to get things done. How many times do we say, "We could achieve X, Y, or Z if we only had more money or had more connections"? How many times do we make excuses about why we can't achieve something? When you don't have money or many resources at your fingertips, use what you do have and use it to your best ability to get what you want out of life. Not having much money or resources forces you to think outside the box, which usually results in an even better way to achieve something.

2. **Build Meaningful Relationships.** Relationships are everything in business and in life. They are what we all are looking for as humans. We want to connect with others and build a bond with them that lasts beyond a business deal or a simple interaction. David showed us how to build meaningful relationships through preparing meals and having dinner together. He showed us how to connect with others on a different level and in a different way. David showed us how he has been able to connect with some of the most influential people in Boston— by showing up, adding massive value, and expecting nothing in return.

3. **Give Your Life Away for the Joy of Others.** The more you give in life, the more you will get in return. I'm not just talking about money. I'm talking about the feeling you get when you give to others. David made many sacrifices to build the Roxbury Youth Orchestra, and because of that, he has created a platform that is supporting youths in achieving their own dreams. He has given them a platform that teaches them things that can relate to all walks of life, and it's preparing them for their future success. Their success becomes David's success. Now that some of his students are all grown up and

fulfilling their own dreams, they are paying it forward for others and are also helping David continue the mission of the Roxbury Youth Orchestra.

Samantha and I left Boston with more relationships and a burning desire to give more to others. We were on a mission to get rid of everything that no longer added value to our lives. We were all in on helping others find their own meaning of success in life.

Chapter 8
Brandon

Selling Everything and Our Next Chapter of the Show

O n Memorial Day, we left Boston and drove nineteen hours over a span of two days back to our house in Garnavillo. On our way back, we stopped in a random town, had breakfast at a local diner, and watched part of a town parade. The days after filming were always fun because we could relax and explore places before having to think about the next city. We always rewarded ourselves with some time together doing random things around the city we were in or in different cities in between our drive to our next destination.

We made it to Cleveland, our halfway point, again so we could stop and visit Jeff Hoffman and update him on our show. We also had the first rough cut of our show trailer. Jeff was impressed that we had literally pulled off filming another full episode of the show in just four weeks. Our previous meeting with him had just happened twenty-eight days earlier and when we'd had that meeting, we had no script and no idea where we were going to live in Boston and what scenes we were going to film. The fact that we pulled that off in that short of a time shows you what is possible when you act. Many people spend weeks or even months planning for a shoot. Most production companies would have taken at least three months to pull that off. We did it in four. How? Because we had no other option, and I made sure to push the team to meet that timeline.

I've never been the easiest person to work with, just ask Samantha or any of our team members. I will say that I do push people to go beyond their own limits and help them achieve things that they would think is impossible. Carlos, one of our sound guys and assistant editors, once told me that it always blew him away how I would frequently throw our team into crazy situations and timelines for filming that we always managed to pull off. Some shoot days went for nineteen hours. We all pulled off these crazy goals because we all believed in the vision. We had become a close family working on a mission together. Each one of us brought something to the table and helped one another work efficiently. I would pick our film crew over any team, any day. No top production team in Hollywood could ever replace them.

After another strategy session with Jeff over breakfast, Samantha and I made the rest of our drive back home to Iowa. Over the next few weeks, we started to give away various items from our house. We would send people pictures of things and ask them if they wanted it. Some bigger items we sold to have some gas money for our next adventure on the road. June 19 was our house-sale closing date, so we had to get rid of as much stuff as possible as soon as possible. We ended up renting out a storage unit to store the remainder of our belongings. As we went through items in our house, many memories arose. This was a reminder that we were letting go of the past and starting a new chapter. Some things were hard to let go, but we both held each other accountable to get rid of things that we otherwise wouldn't.

During the few weeks we were home, we also spent some time with family, and I gained the courage to talk with my father about the idea of me selling the ice business that I had bought from him five years before. My father was still working in the business, yet he was ready to be out of it. The only way I would be able to keep the business going was to run it myself or try to find someone to run it for me, which would be a very difficult task, especially in the ice business. As my father and I talked about me potentially selling it, we cried. It was a very difficult decision to make as my father had started the business in 1986. When I later purchased it from him, I had worked it hard and had no intention of ever selling it, but life changes. Things change. I also never thought I would travel the country and film a TV show. Ten years before, I never thought that I would ever leave my hometown of Garnavillo. Time changes things and in the world we live in, things are always changing. Opportunities come and go. Life will take you down roads that you would have never imagined; but I believe it's a good thing to take roads you have never traveled before instead of taking the same road you have been on your entire life.

June 19 came, and we closed on our house. We dropped off the keys at our real estate agent's office, took one last look at our home, and drove toward Denver, Colorado. We were officially homeless. The only place we knew to go to was our next city on the map. The moment we drove out of Garnavillo was bittersweet. I was scared, excited, and wondering what was going to happen next. The future was unknown. We were on the road and traveling toward our next city to find success.

Chapter 9

Samantha in Denver

Your Story Matters

Thoughts While Driving to Denver

Leaving Iowa, everything started to sink in for me. We had just sold our house, the one place that was home; the place that I loved going back to when we were exhausted from all the travel. KodiKay and I had had a conversation in Austin about the comfort of having a home, a place where you could just be you. I had never looked at our home as a place that I valued until I was on the road as much as we were—especially after the situation we had in the hotel in Austin. After all of this, I realized the importance of having a home and although I know we didn't need the house in Iowa, I was still sad to know that we wouldn't have anywhere to go after filming. There is something about a space that truly shows who you are as a person. Brandon, on the other hand, could literally live in our Tahoe. A dozen times, he brought up the idea of sleeping in the car. That was insane to me, but he really didn't care. If I weren't along on the trip, I think that's where he would have ended up most nights. Thanks to me, he slept in a nice bed. *You're welcome, Brandon!*

When I first met our director, Shawn, to talk about the show, I somehow became so comfortable with him that I blurted out everything about my past. We were at a coffee shop in Winter Park, Florida, brainstorming ideas for the show's storyline. So many things had been kept inside my soul and were now out for others to hear, and this felt both scary and freeing. I could tell that Shawn understood me.

When Shawn spoke to me about my obstacles, it felt like he really knew my pain. I had never thought to talk to someone about these things, but he changed my perspective about this. Holding our worry inside only makes things harder. It creates this story that we aren't worthy enough to become something new, to become everything that we dream of being. And although he sat and listened to me, my thoughts were scaring me. I still had that mindset of my story being a cry out and that I was only looking for attention. I didn't want attention. I just wanted to inspire someone who was going through the same thing. But others' judgment of me was back on my mind, again. How can other people's perspectives literally run our lives? Why do we fear their opinions? I was hoping to figure all of this out as I unraveled my hurtful past. I understood that other people's opinions stop us from doing what we want, yet I was still letting that control what I did, and didn't, want to share with the world.

As Brandon and I drove through Nebraska, we had a deep conversation about sharing my story. I had never thought about my past being part of my story. I was just happy that it was behind me. It was uncomfortable to talk about it in front of anyone besides Brandon. The drug addiction was embarrassing. I had graduated high school late and was known as "the girl who was on drugs." This wasn't something I wanted to promote to the world. It also wasn't easy talking about an eight-year relationship that I had put my entire heart into only to find that we were not right for each other.

Ultimately, I was open to the notion of sharing my story, but I didn't want it to define me again. I had just gotten over that hill. Brandon didn't understand why I found it so hard to talk about my past. He had a solution for every excuse I had to not share it. He acted like he knew the pain that it brought me. He was so focused on making the episode impactful that I felt he was putting my feelings on the back burner. I expressed to him that I felt anxiety when I talked about it. He would just shake his head and tell me that once I talked about it more, I would be fine. He just didn't get it. This led to me feeling angry with Brandon. He hadn't endured what I had, and I was starting to feel like he was forcing me to do something I had no intentions of ever doing.

Continually, Brandon would tell me that I would help so many women. Meanwhile, all I could think of was the fear of what others would think. He wasn't making anything easier, and I felt he was disappointed in me for having so much doubt in myself. I understood that the next episode of our show would be about women's empowerment, but I didn't feel like it was the right time to share something so deep. I was really stuck on what I should and shouldn't share. Our conversation made me upset, and I told him I didn't want to be a part of this episode. He wasn't going to ever understand my feelings. I feared hurting the person who my story was about: the man who had stripped every ounce of strength out of me. I never wanted what happened between us to be a story I shared, but ultimately it was my past and I only am where I am because of it. Again, just like all the previous months, however, my fear of others' judgment was my biggest obstacle.

We had a lot of driving to do so I started to write down my story. I was so unsure that it would even make an impact. *Why do I need to talk about the things that controlled me for so long?* I thought. *I don't want to express the pain I was in to feel worthy.* I suffered deeply from my ex. It was a battle of doing whatever it took to make him happy. I completely changed everything I was in hopes of becoming everything he needed me to be. This had drained my entire soul of happiness. We spent almost every single day together from the age of fifteen until age twenty-three. I scheduled my every move around his emotions. Everything I did for him was done in hopes to stop a fight from happening. He made me feel like the worst person on earth, and all I could do was love him and try to help him control his anger. It's hard when the other person doesn't see the problem. It was the hardest eight years of my life and when I left the guy, I promised myself to never look back.

My story wasn't something I ever thought I would share because I was still suffering from a lot of hurt. The more I thought about my past, the more things I started to realize, which scared the heck out of me. Picking apart my past brought up so many memories that I had muted out of my life for the past five years. These were painful memories that brought up a lot of anger. I had only told a handful of people about what had hurt me the most in life and the thought of being open to tell anyone who would be watching our show scared me. I know my past is the only reason I am who I am today so I should be thankful for it. It just felt so terrifying to share with people who have the right to judge, I guess. I think we can all relate to this fear in some way. So many people spend their lives knocking other people down, and as humans, our feelings get in the way and ultimately others' words make us feel defeated. I feared that some people would define me by my previous drug addiction and for staying with a man who had torn me down. While I knew my story could help others, I couldn't help but find reasons not to share it.

The mountains started to appear, so I knew we were close to Denver. Colorado was breathtaking, and I again was so grateful to experience what it all had to offer. We were lucky enough to stay with our friends Stephen, Katie, and their beautiful bulldog, Hank, for the first week while we searched for an apartment. We had met them only eight months prior and right away became great friends. During our stay with them, they showed us around the city and took us to our first axe-throwing experience. It was challenging, and it didn't help that Katie and I were wearing heels. Regardless, we had fun! She and Stephen were both so supportive of what we were doing with the show, and it was great to have them host us while we got familiar with Denver. For the next couple of days, we hung out and brainstormed more ideas for the show.

Using Fitness to Impact Women

We planned for our Denver show to feature two women in addition to myself. Brandon and I had interviewed two women in the fitness industry on the phone prior getting into the city. Those women and I had all found fitness in different ways, so I was excited to show the world how moving your body can change your mindset no matter why you choose to move. Featuring some great women would not only be inspiring but would hopefully help other women see that fitness can be a huge part of change.

Of the two women, Brandon and I first met up with Jourdan—and her husband, Kit—at a coffee shop in the downtown area. We immediately hit it off with them. They both enjoyed fitness like Brandon and me, and they both were around our age. It was refreshing to hang out with a couple of a similar age and with similar interests. I particularly enjoyed the fact that I could learn from another woman in fitness and get someone else's perspective in this space. Jourdan's story was very inspiring, and she had a wide range of experiences in her career.

Jourdan Baldwin

Jourdan Baldwin graduated from Colorado State University with a health and exercise science degree and with the goal of becoming a personal trainer. She started out training at a twenty-four-hour fitness facility. Soon after training clients, she decided she wanted to do group training for women. At this time, group training wasn't as popular as it is today, so she wasn't sure what to expect. The idea came to her in April, so she put together a summer body challenge for women. She released an ad and to her surprise, fifty-six women signed up. Her event became a huge success!

This success built up her training credibility. She quickly outgrew working at the gym and wound up putting on her own classes at a rundown old baseball center. Jourdan also started to run boot camps in a park in Fort Collins, Colorado. Connections grow when you work out and overcome obstacles together during the workout. Jourdan's boot camps started to build a strong community of women. Beyond working out, the camps also became a networking opportunity for everyone. After class, women would open up to the group and share stories. When you are vulnerable and open up to others, trust and a bond unlike anything else results. What Jourdan created in these groups is truly inspiring.

During this time, Jourdan was presented with the opportunity of a full-time job starting a CrossFit gym in the Middle Eastern country, ironically enough, of Jordan. She accepted the offer and brought Kit with her to help build up the gym. At the time, Kit and Jourdan were only dating. They had worked together in a gym previously, so they felt like this would be a perfect project to take on together.

Living in another country, Jourdan encountered obstacles due to cultural differences. In Jordan, it is considered disrespectful for a woman to look into another man's eyes, so anytime Jourdan was walking down the street, she would look at the ground to avoid eye contact with men. Additionally, women were expected to wear baggy clothes that covered their bodies and didn't show any skin. Others frowned upon a woman wearing shorts or a T-shirt. One day when Jourdan was working out at the gym, she wore what she normally wore in the US: a T-shirt and shorts. Fifteen minutes into the workout, the gym owner told her she needed to put more clothes on. That experience made her realize how different things were for women in Jordan.

One day, she decided she wanted to do something for the women in her class that would make them feel free while working out. Jourdan ordered blinds to cover up all the windows in her classroom so no one could look into the room. Then, right before she started the class, she told all the women to take off their baggy clothes and put on the shorts and tank tops that she had ordered for them. Such a simple outfit is normal for women to wear in the US, but the idea was mind-blowing for women in this country. Throughout the workout, Jourdan could see the women open up. Being dressed in shorts and tank tops was freeing for these women. It was also a monumental moment in Jourdan's career and changed the way she looked at fitness and being open as a woman. It taught her so much about life.

After spending almost two years in the country, Jourdan and Kit were ready to come back to Colorado to pursue their own endeavors. Jourdan's experience abroad had motivated her to go all in on working solely with women in training and boot camps. She eventually partnered with Sarah Fox to put on boot camps and to create the Fresh Fitness app, which provides custom workouts for women and other resources in health and fitness.

Jourdan and Kit eventually got married but in a way they hadn't planned. The week before their wedding, Kit wound up in the hospital with pneumonia. Days later, Jourdan asked the doctor if he could be released for the wedding, and the doctor replied that if Kit left, there was a pretty high chance he could die. I can't even imagine what was going through Jourdan's mind. If that had been me and Brandon, I'm not sure what I would have done.

Luckily, Kit and Jourdan were able to get married right outside the hospital on their wedding day, and Kit got better with time and is as healthy as can be today. This story gave Brandon and me a totally different perspective about getting married and being there for each other in sickness and in health. During their wedding week, Kit and Jourdan worked through one of the biggest obstacles in their lives. Their dilemma made the obstacles that Brandon and I faced with the show seem much smaller. Health is the most important part of our lives, because if we aren't healthy, we can't enjoy any other aspect of our lives.

Brandon and I could relate to Kit and Jourdan's relationship. They both had worked in business together and had traveled together to open a gym in another country. We had traveled together for the show and had worked to make our dream become a reality with the show. We also faced our own obstacles during our trip around the country and before we started our journey for the show. With our wedding only three months away, Jourdan and Kit's wedding experience really hit home with us. Brandon and I were about to take our relationship to an entirely new level by tying the knot in marriage.

After meeting with Jourdan, Brandon and I met with Marie Borquez at yet another coffee shop. I swear we could have won a record for visiting the most coffee shops in a year. Marie shared such an inspiring story about why she was in the fitness industry. She was so nice to both of us! She wanted to help us in any way possible, even if we didn't ultimately choose to feature her on the show. Her motivation to help others overcome their own pain and obstacles came from her own painful experiences growing up and using exercise to deal with her own pain.

Marie Borquez

At seven years old, Marie Borquez found out that she had scoliosis, an abnormal lateral curvature of the spine. The condition can be very painful and disabling and makes regular exercises that others do with ease, difficult. Marie's mom didn't want her daughter to endure surgery at seven years old and get a metal rod placed in her back, so the rest of her family decided to help Marie get through this by trying other outlets such as corrective exercises and staying active to deal with the diagnosis. They motivated her and became her biggest supporters. The doctor prescribed her to stay active to deal with the pain. Her family always told her being active wasn't something she had to do but it was something she would get to do. Instead of having her look at it as a chore, they made her look at it as an opportunity or something fun.

Marie tried out for sports and also got into dance. Dance challenged her—various moves hurt her. At times, she felt stuck. Pain was always a part of her life. Some days, the pain level would be a one or two out of a ten, and other days it could be as high as a level nine. Being in dance made her feel like she could be a part of something. The rhythm and beat lit her up and gave her hope. Dance and music are what she loved. The motion and movement in her body made her feel normal, and the music encouraged her to find that spot in her heart that made her feel like she was going to get through everything.

When she turned eighteen and was on the cusp of going to college, Marie wasn't sure what she wanted to do. She was always passionate about healthcare because of her frequent doctor visits. At first, she thought she wanted to become a nurse. Then she thought she wanted to go into physical therapy. She ended up going to college for exercise science. Her main desire was to help others get through their own struggles just like she had with scoliosis. Eventually, she concluded that she wanted to become a personal trainer and help others become the best version of themselves through the power of fitness.

Scoliosis had taught Marie that everything comes from your core when exercising. She helps her clients find their core in their workouts. Your core is where your spine is, and working your core connects your mind and body. A strong core allows you to dig deeper and connect mentally and emotionally. From her experiences working with women, it also opens them up to share more about themselves and their obstacles in life beyond fitness. You see, working out isn't just about looking good and losing weight. It's about feeling good and overcoming various obstacles. It eliminates fear, and it reduces stress. It motivates you! Marie's mission is to help others find the inner strength or inner athlete that is deep inside them.

Some of the women she trains regularly have kids or have experienced things that made them forget to take care of themselves along the way. They forgot to do the things they used to love doing, like running, playing volleyball, or engaging in any activity that used to be a big part of their lives. Marie's goal is to help them discover that side of themselves again, and she pushes them to do things that allow them to remember what it feels like. Along the way, other emotions may come up from their past, which they can then deal with and talk about. It's more than just being about working out to look good; it's about helping others find themselves again and figuring out who they really are. Fitness gives you structure, energy, and a sense of accomplishment. It's those little wins that turn into big wins down the road.

Marie uses her experiences dealing with pain and hurt from having scoliosis as a way to help others overcome their own pain and obstacles. She could have let scoliosis hold her back from doing the things she wanted, but instead she is doing whatever she wants and is using her experiences to help others. It's truly amazing what fitness can do for a person. Women can see themselves in a different light, and fitness allows them to become stronger. It empowers them to do things on their own.

Fitness allows women to become the best version of themselves, and it empowers them in their daily life. As women, it's important to feel empowered because we want to know we can do things on our own. You can be in the forefront and don't have to be in the background. As a woman, you can lead! When women have community, they feel empowered by having other women to call on.

Hearing Jourdan's and Marie's stories was empowering. These women are making an impact in the communities that they live in. I know how much fitness changed my life, and it was motivating to hear what it had done for them. Both Brandon and I agreed that these women would both be great for the show. Now the work would begin. Picking scenes. Flying our crew into town. Finding them a place to stay. Organizing everything so it would go as smoothly as possible. We were in charge of everything. It was a lot on both of us, but we knew no one would fight for the dream as much as we would.

As the filming date neared, my story continually repeated inside my head. *Am I ready to express my past on camera? Will it really help other women?* I've seen the outcome of other brave women tell their stories and know how much their stories impacted me. I tried to convince myself that what I had endured as a youth had made me who I am today, and that I'm strong and beautiful. Getting to the mindset I have today happened because of all the pain I was once in. Living under someone else's circumstances was draining, and I became numb for the time I was with my ex-boyfriend. So many thoughts swirled in my head. *Maybe it will never feel like the right time. God only gives us what we can handle. I was brought to this moment for a reason.* My team and my fiancé were leading me to live my purpose. I wanted to help women find happiness, and maybe my story would open up the eyes of those women who were hurting.

Two years prior to this time of deep thought, I would have never considered sharing my story. Like, don't even have a camera by me. I hated being on camera, and I especially hated talking about myself. Being with Brandon changed my perspective about being on film because I saw that the power of a story can help so many people. However, the number of times I switched from wanting to share my story to not wanting to share it was too many to count. It was a nonstop battle between me, myself, and I. I just felt that I had finally gotten over that hump of becoming a new person, and I didn't want to bring up something that defined me for so long. It was selfish on my end because it ultimately could help a lot of people. Or so that's what others were telling me.

Filming in Denver

Filming had begun, and I was a mess. I wasn't "on point" at all. I had forced myself into a negative mindset, again. A week prior, I had committed to being a big part of this episode, but as the time came, I just lost it. I was mad at the world. I was mad at Brandon. I was mad at all of the stuff that I had been through. As I wrote down my thoughts and emotions about the addiction that had once controlled me and robbed me of my strength, anger bubbled up. I didn't want to tell the world. I hated Brandon for pushing me to do it. Again, here I was ruining the experience because of the anger I had built up inside of me. I let my emotions control everything. At one point during filming, I called the wedding off and told Brandon I didn't want to see him after this episode. Talk about bad energy in the room. The sad part was that at that time, I meant every word. I wasn't seeing the good in any of it. Why would we let our relationship suffer so badly in hopes of creating the show? Why was he pushing me so much when he knew I was hurting so badly? I couldn't find the answers. I was worried about what was to come after we left Denver.

Every other month, I'd had to put on my big girl pants and roll with it, even if that meant I needed to force myself to do it. I felt if I didn't complete the episode, I would fail the team. I didn't want them to look at me as a failure. Heck, I'm sure they already had enough thoughts about the bad attitude I was bringing. Throughout the year, the guys had seen every single side of me. I wasn't proud, but things were what they were. It didn't help that a team of men surrounded me. I needed emotional support, something that was hard to get without having one of my girl-friends around. Ladies, you know what I mean!

For one of the scenes, we filmed Jourdan and her business part-ner Sarah while they went through one of their group classes. I was excited to move my body, and the film crew was focused more on the entire group instead of just me. This gave me a break from overthinking what I had to say. After the workout, we sat in a circle and shared our thoughts about life and our obstacles. The moment was really defining for me, something that really changed my perspective on sharing my story. After everyone was done talking, a sweet girl approached me and said how much she could relate and that she was once addicted to meth as well. She was so genuine and appreciative of me talking about some-thing so dark. At that moment, I realized that I'm not the person who needs to hear what I have to say. Others do. It made me realize that I'm being selfish. The fact that this girl could come up to me and relate and share what she had endured was the best feeling in the world.

After that conversation, my thoughts started to shift—not perma-nently, but I was really trying to live with gratitude. I don't know why we continually live off negativity when the miracles around us are much more beautiful. The following day, Brandon and I drove to Boulder to hike Flat Iron with the whole crew. This was one of the many experiences that we got to work on together as a team, which always brought us closer. Pictures online matched what was right in front of us—the blue sky, the dirt paths, the mountains. It was early, but I was ready because this was going to be a powerful scene introducing *my why*.

We met at the bottom of the mountain and went over what we wanted to capture. We wanted to reference the obstacles that I had overcome while climbing a mountain, and Shawn had the best ideas. As we made our way up the hill, we filmed multiple scenes. The climb really expressed what my life was and what it had become. We worked together perfectly, and as we did, so much pressure lifted from my shoulders. I hadn't felt this comfortable during filming before, which assured me that I was here for a reason. It was a journey to get to this mindset of feeling worthy enough to share my past, but I needed those obstacles so that I could discover my true potential. Oh, and the views were breathtaking. It was surreal and worth the five-hour hike!

Before this experience, I had been so concerned about what others would think of me. But I don't have that concern anymore. It's ridiculous to even think about that now. We *all* endure experiences that are meant to teach us things. We have the ability to dig into what is happening and learn from it. We can choose not to but, in my opinion, we are then living in a place that doesn't fulfill us. We are given hard times to learn from them. Other people's negative opinions mean absolutely nothing. They only hold us back from greatness, so finding a way to ignore them is important. They will try to speak louder and louder, but luckily, we have the capability to say, "I can't hear you."

Not everyone needs to respect me. Not everyone needs to support me. I've learned that I am the only author of my story. I'm the only one living every single chapter of my life. What an incredible feeling. If I want the world to know my ups and downs, then I will share them. I'm not living for anyone else anymore. I'm living for me, and I know that I will make a difference in someone's life. It doesn't need to be millions of people. It just needs to be someone. Life is short. It's our duty to help others as much as we can.

Other people's stories have helped me realize so much about myself and how much I can relate to others. In a world filled with so much judgment and fear, just know that your story will make a difference. People need to hear more about the good that is taken from such dark places. It wasn't easy for me, but I have a new view on the power of a story. We can sit back and let others' opinions stop us from helping others, or we can share what our experiences have taught us and change the outcome of someone else's life.

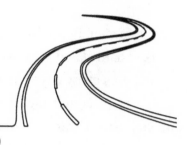

Chapter 10
Samantha

My Story Matters

I want to give you an inside look of my story so that you can better understand why I endured so many challenges during the filming of the show. As we were filming, Brandon encouraged me to share obstacles that I had dealt with in my past, and as he did, I struggled to find my worth in sharing my story. Among other things, I'd had trouble fitting in with what I saw as more successful people (a struggle I endured while filming the show and in my life before it). I'm sure some of you can relate to this, and I hope you can find the strength to move forward from it and really dig into what the good is in every situation. From here, I am going to lay out for you where my struggles originated from.

Growing up with four sisters, I had some great childhood memories. We were all very close in age and did everything together. My mother ran a daycare as well, so we always had about fifteen kids in our house most weekdays. The creativity was endless, and being around so many kids was something I always looked forward to. That very creativity led me to one of my hobbies, gymnastics. I started it at four years old and immediately fell in love with the sport. It was the first thing that I worked hard at and got rewarded for. I wanted to become the best, and I spent hours every day trying to perfect my skills.

I started competing at a young age. I enjoyed the challenge, but looking back I was so hard on myself when I didn't compete perfectly. In gymnastics, you are judged not only on your skills but on your routines and your ability to stick every single move. Eventually, I worked my way to my dream gymnastics team, and I found myself performing with girls I had once looked up to. It was an accomplishment that I had worked so hard to achieve, and that year of competing when I was thirteen years old was one of the most rewarding and challenging years of my life. Gymnastics taught me that hard work and consistency can take you anywhere you choose to go and that not giving up can put you in a place where you always dreamed of being.

As much as I loved being a gymnast, however, it slowly became something I didn't want for myself anymore. That choice was driven by hanging out with the wrong people and doing drugs. I didn't know how much regret and disappointment I would have from quitting the one thing I loved most in exchange for a life that almost killed me. I was young. I didn't know that a sentence such as "Do you want to try this?" would put me on a spiraling path of self-destruction and hurting the people I loved the most. Sure, I had a new group of friends, but I wasn't chasing my dream anymore. I was chasing a high that forced me to become someone I hated. All the determination I once had was gone, and all of my energy was being put toward finding money to keep my high going. I couldn't help who I was back then, and that is the hardest part. If I had just stayed focused on gymnastics, then none of the obstacles that later appeared on my path would have been there. But that wasn't the case. At the age of fourteen, I became addicted to meth.

The next year challenged me. I was no longer associated with being on the top team in gymnastics. I was put into a category with other drug addicts and, sadly, I became a really mean human being. I didn't care about anything or anyone. Whatever it took to get high, I did it, whether that meant stealing from my parents or friending drug dealers to get free drugs. At that time, we would mostly use cocaine, ecstasy, and meth. We would usually take turns buying for the entire group, which was not cheap, so finding ways to get money was a priority. I would lie to my parents about needing clothes or food money and go behind their backs to buy drugs. I became a completely different person during that year. I lost all control of who I was, and it destroyed my mindset. When I didn't have money to stay high, I would spiral down into a deep depression and become so angry.

When I was around all my friends who were also high, I always felt so alone. Sure, I thought I was having the time of my life, but at the end of the day, I felt suffocated in a body that was filled with chemicals that essentially could have killed me time over time. Yet at the same time, I couldn't see myself functioning without these drugs or friends. Addiction can happen so fast, especially when that is all you surround yourself with. As time passed, I was introduced to more and more dealers, and this gave me more access to purchase whatever I wanted. My main choice was meth, but some days I would take ecstasy on top of the meth. I have no idea how my tiny body made it through everything that I put it through, but I thank God that it did.

Addiction led me to break the law in many different ways. I was smoking cigarettes, drinking, and running away from home almost every night. Because I was fourteen, my parents struggled with disciplining me. I was choosing to disobey them and find ways to get out of the house. I found myself on probation and going to court for underage drinking tickets. Somehow, with the hundreds of days of having meth in my pocket, I never got caught. I was with other people who got caught, but I never had anything on me those specific times. I was messed up when I ran into the law, and a small part of me felt like the authorities saw my pain and secretly wanted me to wake the heck up. I'm sure seeing such a young girl with a group of guys who had no reason to be with me was suspicious, but the police never took me home unless I was intoxicated. That was the beauty of meth. I learned how to control myself in front of authority, and so for the time, I was able to make myself less noticeably high.

I struggled in school. I made it to a couple of classes a week and spent all day at a drug dealer's house getting high. While on meth, time flew. Sometimes I wouldn't even realize that a week had passed by because we would stay up playing cards as the clock ticked. Sometimes we would be so high that I forgot about the outside world. We spent a lot of time trying to find ways to pay for our drugs. One of the most sickening things we would do when we ran out of meth was search the floors of the entire house that we were in in hopes that we had dropped a small crystal. We would put anything that looked like meth in our pipes and smoke it, even if it was literally a rock. It disgusts me to think about that, but that was my life and my normal back then.

At this time in my life, I found myself weighing eighty-nine pounds. When I discovered this at a regular doctor's visit, my mother and I were shocked. I remember Mom telling me that I hadn't weighed that little in a long time. I looked so fragile, and I know it had everything to do with the drugs. It was an interesting feeling when I knew deep inside that I was not making the right choices, yet I still chose to do the opposite of what I needed. I felt invincible yet scared. Things slowly started to go even more downhill. People were talking in school about how cracked up I looked, and I started to become embarrassed. I started questioning myself and the people around me and if they were really my friends. I was always giving every penny I had for us all to get high, and I felt that without the money, I wouldn't have any friends.

I remember the moment that changed my outlook on my situation so clearly. We were all hanging out and had decided to trip on mushrooms. I had done them before but never while on meth. To make things even more dramatic, we decided to take ecstasy as well. I remember being in the bathroom looking in the mirror and seeing someone so messed up. Everyone was dancing and having a great time, but all I could think about was how my heart was literally beating outside of my body. I mean, you could see how slow it was beating. I was so tiny that I could see my heart beating through my shirt. Everyone kept telling me that it was crazy cool, but I was scared. I left that party and I went home and lay on the sofa chair. I looked at the wall, and it was moving so fast. I closed my eyes and heard my dad walk downstairs to go to work. I held my eyes shut so tight until he left and for the first time, I prayed that I would fall asleep and wake up sober.

I was experiencing so many emotions, and I so badly wanted to feel normal again. That day at school, I went to my counselor and confessed that I was using meth and that I needed help. I was crying my eyes out and telling her everything. She put me in her car and drove me home, where I told my mom that I wanted to die and that I was so far gone with my life. For the first time, I saw my mom cry and it just hit me. I couldn't live that life anymore. I didn't want to feel alone, and I didn't want to depend on drugs to get through the day. That day saved my life because it forced me to open up to someone who actually cared and listened. That one incident where my heart was beating slowly brought me back to reality. I stayed inside for what seemed like a long time. The thought of getting ahold of any drug that would put me back to where I was terrified me. Luckily, and I don't say that lightly, I have never touched meth again. How? I have no idea. I know how crazy that sounds that I didn't go to treatment, but I truly feel I scared myself out of addiction. I continued to smoke weed and drink, but I wasn't addicted to those things. I just used them recreationally. But while I somehow found myself clear of my meth addiction, I soon found myself in a relationship that stripped every ounce of strength from my body that I had just gained back.

Though I was over my addiction, it was still taking a toll on every aspect of my life. I was very fragile to what I should be feeling and to what I should be focusing on. At the time, I didn't know what was right for me and the timing of this new relationship was perfect. Perfect in a way that I needed something to keep my mind off the big black hole I had just dug myself out of. And perfect in a way that I felt someone really cared about me.

Our relationship was equivalent to any high school relationship—a lot of drunk nights, smoking marijuana, and skipping school. I actually moved in to his house when I was in tenth grade and spent almost every minute and night with him until we were twenty-three. I look back at that whole scenario of me living with him when I was fifteen and think, *How in the world did his parents let that happen?* But that was our life, and at the time we loved it.

Soon, I came to realize that he would become angry with me pretty easily—especially when I found out he was sleeping with other girls and lying about who he was hanging out with. Again, we were in high school, so I felt like these things happened all the time. Love wasn't something that teenagers focused on. One clear memory I have is of me waiting at my front door for him to pick me up. I remember my father telling me that he wasn't going to show up, and I still stood there until it was time to go to bed. I loved him so much and didn't realize that what was right in front of me was wrong. Wrong in a way that from the beginning he did not respect me. I wasn't his priority. I would question him the next day and find out that he had been with another girl.

The situation angered him more than it angered me, so at the end of the fight, I would be the one saying sorry. This happened for eight years, and yet I still begged for his love and attention. I forgave him for every argument we had, and so whatever was behind us was just that. It wasn't until I left him that I got to look at our entire eight years together, which led to *a lot* more anger and pain. I let all of that happen, and the hardest part was knowing that I couldn't help myself back then.

As our relationship grew "stronger," and I put that in quotation marks for a reason, I completely lost myself again. I didn't lose myself in a way that I lost myself with drugs but actually in the complete opposite way. Drugs made me happy. They made my real life disappear, and I was living on cloud nine. This relationship made me sad and angry. I was living with so much heartache and shame. I spent almost every day terrified. Yet every single day I still loved him as much as day one. No matter how unimportant he made me feel or how many times he told me I would become *nothing*, I still loved him.

For the next couple of years, our life revolved around arguments and fighting, and I removed myself from the relationship several times. The times that I did this filled me with so much power from within. At one point, he had kicked me out of our Orlando apartment (he was going to school there) and my dad bought me a plane ticket home. I was so proud of myself and within days, he messaged me three heart-tugging words: *I miss you*. I tried to fight going back so bad. I had it in my head that I was done. Yet something inside my head allowed him to get me a ticket to go back to him. Even my parents were confused because I had been so sure about never seeing him again. I can't even count how many times he told me to leave—hundreds of times. And there I was at his doorstep after every single argument.

When I came back that specific time, I flew into Orlando in the late afternoon. He was going to pick me up after not seeing me for a week. I was slightly scared because I never knew what his attitude would be. I was standing on the baggage claim floor, and he must have been on the departing flights floor waiting for me. I kept calling him and was so confused about whether he was even there or not. He called me back and was instantly angry. Suddenly, fear overwhelmed me. *No, no, no, why did I come back?* I thought. After finally finding each other, I could tell he was not happy. As we drove away, he told me how stupid I was and that he didn't even want me back. At one point, he turned around to take me back to the airport. Honestly at that point, I was just so used to how he treated me that I was numb. I started to cry and begged for him to just take us home. I wasn't crying because he was mad though. I was crying because my parents were right.

I spent eight years of my life catering to him. I cooked his meals, did his laundry, and cheered him on while he went to college. I sat home preparing whatever it was he needed to make his life as easy as possible. At only nineteen years old, I felt like a robot. I barely did anything for myself. I would bring his meals to him during college and if I was even one minute late, he would become furious and not eat. I was not his girlfriend; I was his maid. If his life wasn't happy, mine wasn't either. He was so hard to please, and for the entire time I was with him, that's all I wanted to do.

He was also addicted to marijuana. Now I know marijuana can be used in many positive ways these days so I'm not against it, but what he made me do is what was wrong. He had anxiety and couldn't leave the house without pot. We barely ever did things outside the house, but I was okay with that because it almost always led to him being mad at me. Whether my shorts were too short (which I stopped wearing to avoid an argument) or another man was looking at me, I would rather just stay at home so that I didn't get blamed for his anger. The problem with his addiction was that I was the one who had to get the marijuana for him. It was the only thing that calmed him down and if he didn't have it right when he needed it, I wouldn't even come out of the bedroom. I had to friend guys in Orlando to make sure he didn't go without it. I mean like go to stranger's houses *alone* to get something that *he* needed. He never once thought about how dangerous that was. He never once stepped back and thought, *Wow, this girl probably shouldn't be meeting a drug dealer at ten p.m. in the middle of a state that we aren't even from.* He was always thinking about himself, and I did whatever he asked because I felt he might love me more if I did.

I could detail more memories of him, but I'm just going to leave you with one. It's one of the memories that I think about most whenever he crosses my mind. Why did I continue to love him? Why did the pain he gave me not open up my eyes? If you have experienced something like this, I hope that you too can use it as fuel to become more than what happened to you.

So, the memory: It was 2011. We were in my hometown for Christmas, and we always stayed at a hotel when we visited with our three dogs. We decided to go out to a bar with some of our friends from high school. My ex had a temper, but when he was drinking that temper rose to another level. When we would drink together, we would drink a lot of liquor. I think I did shots to numb my pain. Anyway, I remember seeing a guy friend from high school and he told me he had just got engaged. His fiancée was also at the bar, and I was so happy for him. I hugged him and went on with my night. I didn't feel any tension between my then-boyfriend and me at the bar, which was always a good sign. At the end of the night, we took a cab back to the hotel, and that is where things took a turn.

He became violently angry with me for hugging that friend. This shocked me. I thought, *You have got to be kidding me.* I always felt like he would just find reasons to scream in my face. He really loved to belittle me when he was drinking. He was usually pretty intoxicated when it got this bad, so I always just stayed silent and let him yell. This night, his voice became louder and louder, and he slammed me onto the bed and forced me to have sex with him. I was crying my eyes out and begging him to stop, but he didn't care. He wanted to hurt me. I deserved it for congratulating my friend for his engagement. Right?

When everything was over, he packed my bags and threw them out the patio door into the 0-degree winter night. I was so weak from fighting with him that I just left and was sitting outside at two a.m., freezing. I don't like sharing these kinds of stories because I *let* them happen to me. I hid my life from everyone. I let him think that his behavior was normal. To this day, I feel terrible when I tell others about my experiences with him because I don't want to hurt *him*. But this was once my reality and my feelings. I wound up calling his parents. I had no one else to call.

I couldn't call my family because they didn't know the extent of the life I was living. Both of his parents were in the car when they arrived to get me at about two thirty a.m. How embarrassing. Not much was said, but I do recall his mom asking me why he did these things. That was it. Right after we arrived at their house, I went to bed. Not once did I receive a call from my then-boyfriend asking where I was though he knew how cold it was outside.

The next morning, I went back to the hotel to pack up to go home. He was still sleeping. Imagine that. He asked me where I was, and I looked at him with huge eyes. Of course, he didn't remember anything. That was his excuse every single time. With anger and tears, I explained every detail to him. He apologized, and we held each other. He was mad and sad at the same time. If you've ever been in a relationship like this, you can understand exactly how that works.

Soon after all of this, the one thing on his mind was that we needed to go get the morning-after pill so I wouldn't become pregnant. Sadly, that was my reality a lot. He would take me to Walgreens, hand me his debit card, and I would purchase that pill. That happened more than I would like to admit. He never remembered the abuse nor the fear in my eyes as he held me down. And actually, at that point, I didn't think of it as abuse. I just saw it as my life. My heart hurt so bad, but it always did, so I always just let it go. I let myself down that day as I remember telling myself while I was sitting in the freezing cold that I was *done*. Done with these games. Done with getting treated like I was this terrible human being. I did everything for this guy, and everyone knew it besides him. This behavior lasted another two years.

Then one day came when my heart just couldn't take it anymore. I was mentally and physically exhausted. I was extremely weak on the outside and broken on the inside. Often, I asked myself what I had done to put myself in the exact situation I was in. How did the last eight years go by and I still loved him? I still wanted to be with him. I wanted to be the one who changed him to love me back. Whenever I hear the word "heartbreak," it takes me back to those eight years of my life. My heart wasn't literally broken, but it constantly hurt from the sadness and fear that I always felt. It was a pain that was always there, especially when the rooms of our house were filled with anger and fear.

I remember the day I left. The night before, we had gotten in an argument that led me to sleep on the guest bedroom floor. I stayed up thinking about how I could pull myself together and find the strength to leave the relationship. I mean that is what he wanted. He wanted me gone. It had been eight years of me telling myself that I wanted more. I was so scared, and the vision of me living without him made me sick. *How can I leave him and the dogs?* I thought. *They need me. They can't survive without me.*

The next morning, I woke up and went into the bathroom and I could just feel the negative energy in the house. I looked in the bathroom mirror and told myself to pack the car and go. I was thinking, *You said you want more for yourself. You want to find who you really are without the burden of someone who tears you down*. And that was how I left. I started packing my car and between those twenty-plus trips down the stairs and to my car, I don't think he turned around to ask me what I was doing once. At the moment, it broke my heart that he couldn't care less about what I was doing; but now, I understand that because he didn't question me, I was able to leave and become free.

I finished packing up as much as I could and made my way to my family home in Winona. I cried the entire way home and had "A Little Bit Stronger" on repeat for two hours. That was one of the hardest days of my life. My "normal" was taking care of him and living with someone who talked down to me for who I was. The stories he put into my head took every ounce of love and strength out of me and became my life for so long. In the months after I left, I was still in love with him. I missed him so much, but I rarely showed that to him. He didn't understand why I left, and I hope now he can see. I left because I wanted to be happy again. I left because his words left me in constant pain. I didn't leave because I didn't love him. I left so that both of us could live different lives. Happy lives.

As I lay in bed at my parents' house, I thought about what I could do to find that next thing that would consume my heart and mind. A relationship wasn't it. I wanted to do something that would transform who I was and the way that I thought. I wanted to think for myself again. Without the drugs. Without the approval of another person.

I started to run around the city of Winona. Quickly, it became a goal to run ten miles a day. I was still so fragile, depressed, and anorexic, but the feeling of running was so freeing. I hadn't felt free in so long. This led me to lift weights, and I was so surprised about how I felt after a workout. I was intentionally transforming my body—not just the outside, but my entire soul. This allowed me to erase any pain that I had during that time of activity, and I found it to be everything I needed at that time. It was the start of me really digging into how I could help others through fitness. It allowed me to overcome my past because I used every ounce of pain that I had to become the strongest person that I know. I fight hard to be the best for myself and if I hadn't found fitness, I don't think I would have been able to move on like I did. Fitness is the reason that I have found success today.

Everyone uses their past in different ways. Some let it stop them from greatness. Some use it as fuel to become more than they ever imagined. It's ultimately a choice. But what makes that choice so hard? Why don't we choose the better option for ourselves? We know that the past can't be changed. Yet we find ourselves looking back more than we ever look forward. That's because our past is all we know. We know we are hurt from it. We know that it is holding us back, and we know it can't be changed. The future is something we don't know. We don't know what our lives will become if we do move forward. We like things that are comfortable. Being vulnerable and open is extremely uncomfortable until you realize how relatable you are to other people when you open up. That's where life and happiness change. At one point of telling your story, you feel embarrassed, sad, and lost, and then someone speaks up and tells you that they can relate and that you helped them change their way of thinking.

When I started speaking up about my past and the struggles that came with it, I started to realize so much about myself. I learned that my past cannot be changed. I learned that we all have a choice to grow from a time in our lives that seemed unbearable. I learned to use the pain to become the very best version of myself. Pain can tear us down, but if you can build yourself up to use that pain as a reminder of how strong you are, then you will start to accomplish so much more in life. Use it as the fuel to prove to yourself that you are going to achieve that dream of yours. Use it to prove to yourself that you are enough. Once you gain that self-love and that motivation to use all the hurt in your body to push forward, you will start to inspire and motivate others to do the same. We all have struggles, and we all have pain. It's up to *us* and only *us* to power through the hurdles and become everything we aspire to be.

No matter how much I have grown, the year on the road filming *Success in Your City* with Brandon tested me. I experienced all sorts of emotions, and I struggled to live up to that strong person I had found myself to be. It was challenging, and I wanted to quit many times. No matter how much pain I was in, I took away so much more, and I'm thankful I get to share the obstacles from not only my past but from what I deal with every day. No matter how much we have changed, we still deal with hardship and pain every day. I know to choose positivity, but sometimes that negative talk just consumes you and you feel so stuck. I've had a mixture of happy and sad tears while filming the TV show with Brandon, and I hope that you can see a little bit of me in you and go out and find your own version of success.

Chapter 11

Brandon

Overcoming Obstacles

Throughout life, we all encounter obstacles and different seasons that bring us pain and suffering. Life isn't always easy and if it were, what fun would that be? Without struggle, how could we prepare for bigger opportunities that lie ahead? If things always went our way, we wouldn't appreciate the wins as much. When you work hard for something and give it everything you've got, you experience a rewarding feeling when you *do* eventually achieve your goal. The success that comes from the pain, sweat, and tears is what pushes us to get better every single day and get closer to our goals. As humans, we are fulfilled by growth and improving ourselves. Even if we don't reach our big goals, what matters is that we get better and learn in the process of going after them.

In every single city that Samantha and I lived in, we had our own individual struggles. We both had our own ways of dealing with them too. I always felt like I needed to stay strong for both of us and hold it all in, because if I showed weakness, I felt that Samantha or anyone else on our team would lose hope. Samantha expressed her emotions regularly, and sometimes I didn't know how to react to them. I always wanted to be there for her and to comfort her, but sometimes I also didn't want to admit how bad things were as we were going through the trenches and striving to achieve our goal of creating a TV series that we could share with the world.

When we first started our show journey in Scottsdale, we had many great things going for us, but we also faced many unknowns. We didn't know exactly how the show was going to be shot, we didn't know how we would act on camera as characters in the show, and we didn't know how good or bad the show would look. We just knew we had to move forward. We all face unknowns in life, and we fear what we don't know. On our journey, what Samantha and I have discovered is that when you step into the unknown you grow and you learn. You become better and make fewer mistakes. Things are not going to be perfect at first, but that's alright. With learning comes strength and wisdom, which are very valuable.

Experiencing Obstacles

In Austin, Samantha and I had faced the biggest obstacle we had ever encountered together as a couple. Prior to going to that city, if we had known that all of those things were going to happen to us, we probably wouldn't have gone. But because we stepped into the unknown and put ourselves in a position where we were forced to learn and figure things out, we grew in the process. We became stronger. This brought Samantha and me together. If we hadn't been stuck in that hotel broke and wondering what to do next, we wouldn't have gone to Riverbend Church and found God. If that hadn't happened, Samantha and I wouldn't have formed the bond we have now. That low moment in Austin allowed us to come together stronger than ever. It's like the old saying that goes, "What doesn't kill you makes you stronger." I'm sure that we all have had those moments where we thought there was no way out and that the world was coming to an end. But guess what? It's not! Those moments make us who we are. Now, when something goes wrong in Samantha's and my life, we just say, "Well, there must be a reason this is happening. What can we learn from this, and how can we get better?"

After overcoming our obstacles in Austin and filming the next episode, we felt like we could accomplish anything. We felt like we had all the power in the world. At one time or another, many people experience this feeling when they achieve something they have worked hard for. When actors win a huge award or make a lot of money from a role they play, they feel invincible. They feel on top of the world. But what goes up must also come down. That high won't last forever. How you deal with the high matters, and how you deal with going down matters just as much. Some people will come off their high and shoot back down to rock bottom and sometimes never recover. Some of the most successful people of our time have hit rock bottom and used that low time to fuel them back to the top. After getting enough wins in life, you will realize that the ups and downs are just a part of the game, and the next low moment won't take you back as much.

Reflecting on Life and Where to Go Next

During our time in Iowa before heading to Boston, I knew there would be major changes ahead, I just didn't know what would all come with that. Many thoughts were going through my head like *Should I be in the ice business anymore? Should I continue with the Young Entrepreneur Convention?* and *Do we even need the things that we have?* Samantha and I both started to question our own lives and how we were living them. We started to question what success even meant to us. We started to think about our fast-approaching wedding, and we were also thinking about how we would finish out the show.

Spending time in Boston helped solidify our thoughts and wants. It gave us a totally different perspective on life and what matters. I believe we all should gain perspectives from others who live lives that differ from ours. Go learn from people in a different area of business or from people who have a totally different perspective on life. When you put yourself in someone else's shoes, you will gain clarity and come away with a better understanding about why others think and act the way that they do. Samantha and I interviewed many people in Boston for our Boston Ballers podcast series. This experience gave us a wide range of perspectives about business, life, and love. Spending time with David France made us realize that material things aren't that important and without them we could still be fulfilled. In life, it's the little things that matter, and those little things are the memories that stay with us forever.

Boston and its citizens gave us the clarity we needed to go home, sell our house, give away most of our things, sell a business, and even take the next step of me considering selling the family ice business. None of this would've happened if we hadn't gained the experiences we did in Scottsdale, Austin, Iowa, and Boston. You see, everything builds off of the next thing, and each thing builds this bigger picture of who we are and who we want to become. For Samantha and me, it all started with journeying through the unknown. After the unknown came the struggle and the feeling of defeat. After getting through that defeat came the high of feeling invincible and being able to accomplish anything. Through that came the thoughts of what success really means and what we really want our lives to be. Those thoughts combined with more experiences and feedback from others continued to solidify our desires and mission in life.

We all must go through these stages to achieve the bigger things in life. We must go through these stages to continue our constant growth and learning. This process will continue throughout our entire lives, but the unknowns, struggles, obstacles, successes, and new beginnings will take different forms in different directions.

Communication in a Relationship

As Samantha and I drove out of Iowa, knowing we no longer had a house to return to, we experienced a new unknown. Samantha's feelings weren't the same as mine, because as she has told you, I could live out of our Tahoe. I seriously could. As long as I have food, water, and something to sleep in, I'm good to go.

After leaving Iowa, we arrived in Denver, where we had many fun moments, and Samantha and I enjoyed ourselves together—that is, we did when it didn't have to do with Samantha sharing her story and confronting her past. When that subject came up, she found it difficult to talk about. I always encouraged her to share her story because I knew it could help many other women in the world. I also encouraged her to share it because I knew it would help her overcome her past. I can't sit here and say I have any idea of what it felt like to go through what Samantha went through. I have no idea, nor will I ever know. Because of that, it was difficult for Samantha to handle the fact that I was pushing her to share her past.

Filming the Denver episode was probably one of the most challenging parts of our relationship yet because Samantha expressed a lot of anger and resentment when she talked about her story on camera. She had built up so much anger from her past and throughout the year while we traveled and filmed the show. A lot of memories of pain and suffering came up for Samantha and with it came a lot of anger and acting out, which would be expected given everything she had been through. At the time, I tried to be the best fiancé I could be. I know what I may have said or done wasn't probably the best way to handle the situation, but at the time I did the best I thought I could do. We all make mistakes and we all deal with things differently. Samantha dealt with the situation in the way she knew how to at the time, and I dealt with it in the way I knew how to.

We all have our own ways of coping with undesirable things that have happened to us or are happening to us in the moment. I am sharing this because in a relationship or marriage, we need to better understand our significant other and try to put ourselves in their shoes when they are dealing with their own problems or past. Instead of disagreeing with them and forcing them to act and think the way that we do, work to understand them and let them know you are on their side while they are getting through the problem. The better you can communicate and talk through things, the sooner they will be resolved. By no means do Samantha and I have this mastered, but the experience in Denver with her sharing her story on camera definitely taught us many valuable lessons that help us in our relationship today.

After the Denver experience, Samantha and I started to make more decisions together and communicate through them. In prior months, I had, unilaterally, always said we were going to do something, and I would make decisions without asking Samantha. We had concluded that Nashville was going to be the last city we traveled to for the show and that we would get an apartment in Minneapolis after the wedding so Samantha could be closer to her family. The fact that we were only going to visit one more city for the show kind of made me feel defeated, given we had set out to visit twelve cities and were now only doing five. Sometimes I don't understand boundaries and what I feasibly can or cannot do. That's why it's helpful when Samantha brings me back to reality to see what is actually feasible. If she wasn't there to bring me back to reality time to time, I would run myself into the ground.

Working to Cross the Finish Line

Before getting a place to live in Nashville, Samantha and I made some unexpected trips that were necessary to help us fund the rest of the show without taking away from our wedding fund. Our first stop: back to Austin. There I gave a keynote speech at Ricky and KodiKay's annual Mega Agent Mixer event. After Austin, we drove back to Denver, where we did a commercial shoot for Dan Gomer, a local real estate agent who had attended our *Success in Your City* mastermind event while in Denver. Dan's perspective on life and business aligned with ours, and he ended up becoming an associate producer of the Denver episode. Our shoot with Dan was our only commercial shoot in 2018. We had spent the entire year filming the show, and I had turned down other commercial shoots to focus on the show. These few gigs solidified that we only wanted to work with people who we liked and trusted and that we weren't going to do jobs just for the money. When you work with people who have values similar to yours, doing business with them is a much better experience. Your clients become your friends.

When we moved into our Nashville apartment on August 24, there were only twenty-four days before we would film the episode there and fifty days remaining before our wedding. Talk about the ultimate finale of the year for our lives and the show. On top of that, our wedding was being filmed for the show. Samantha and I were about to be confronted with our biggest obstacle of the year and had no option but to succeed. More than 130 people planned to visit us on our special day, and we had yet to figure out how we were going to pull it all off. I'm sure any couple planning a wedding feels that way. Since Samantha basically planned our entire wedding, I will let her share her experience putting it all together. Let's just say that she was the wedding planner and I was the TV show planner. While in Nashville, she spoke about the wedding and I spoke about the show. When we did talk about the wedding, I talked about the different shots our camera crew could capture during the ceremony.

Nashville was our favorite city of the year because we both love country music and also had our first special moment together as a couple in Nashville five years before. Since we loved country music so much and Nashville is full of musicians, we decided to feature a country singer named Faydra Lagro in this episode. She is a woman we had heard two years before when we traveled through the city on our way to Orlando. Faydra and Samantha had hit it off right away, and Samantha was superexcited to share Faydra's story on our show.

Faydra Lagro

Faydra Lagro grew up in Superior, Wisconsin. She got into music when she was in the first grade. Her parents couldn't believe it when she came home one day and told them she had been selected for the solo for her Christmas concert. That's because no one else in her family had any kind of music background. When she was a kid, her parents took her to Nashville, and she played at the Ryman Auditorium, former home of the Grand Ole Opry. She had told her parents that one day she would come back and work full time as a musician. That dream stuck with her as she continued playing music.

Just two weeks before graduating high school, one of her favorite teachers asked her to come back to his office. What he was about to tell her would stop her in her tracks. He said, "What's this I hear you are going to school for music?" She said, "Yeah, I'm so excited. I can't believe I got accepted, and I passed my audition!" He said, "I don't know what you're doing. You are way too smart to be throwing your talent away. You could be a surgeon. You could be a lawyer. You could do anything. You have the brain for it. People would kill to be as smart as you are, and you are just gonna throw it all away?" That comment took the wind right out of her and made her question herself and her decision. The person she looked up to had basically just told her that she was wasting her time by going after music for a career.

Despite her teacher's advice, she enrolled in college to gain a degree in music. In her last year, she became part of a well-known band in the Minneapolis and St. Paul, Minnesota, areas. She had made the commitment to be a full-time musician. It was 2013, and she told herself that she would move to Nashville by 2015 no matter what. Since Nashville is the city of music, she knew she had to be there to take her career seriously.

The year 2015 came, and she was looking at new apartments with her mom in the Minneapolis area. While doing this, her mother reminded her about her desire to move to Nashville and mentioned that maybe she should follow through with that. That's what Faydra had needed to hear; those words prompted her to decide to finally move to the city of her dreams. Soon after this decision, her older sister and cousin helped her pack up her stuff. They loaded it all into a horse trailer and moved her to Nashville. After dropping her off at her new place in the city, she hugged them goodbye. She walked back into her apartment, surrounded by a bunch of boxes. She was in a new city where she knew no one and felt like she was all alone. It was scary and exciting.

Instead of unpacking boxes, Faydra grabbed her guitar, sat on the floor, and played and wrote a song that she now calls "Count Down." The song is about getting up and going somewhere even if you have fears. It's happening and it's happening fast, but no matter how fast it's happening, it's been on your mind for years. You are supposed to be here. It's scary right now. It's uncomfortable. It's not as planned out as it should have been, but you are here. You left everything behind, you are coming, and you're not faltering on that journey. Your whole entire life led to this, no matter how spontaneous you feel in that moment.

This song has so much truth in it. It reminded Samantha and me of our entire journey throughout the year. We were never really ready for the journey or filming the show, but we did it and it all felt spontaneous. We were nervous and scared at times, but we kept moving forward. Our entire lives had led us to the journey around the country. We all experience these moments. Just remember that everything that has happened to you and everything you have worked for has led you to where you are today. Embrace it. Live in the moment. Go with it.

Faydra's first year in Nashville was the hardest. She played at every bar she could, and she started working serving jobs, which allowed her to figure out who did the bookings for certain venues. Figuring this out allowed her to book gigs with them on Nashville's Broadway. Now, she has played almost nightly at places such as Mellow Mushroom, The Saloon, The Stage, Legends, Nashville Underground, and Margaritaville, which is her favorite. This is the same place where Samantha and I first saw Faydra play in 2016. Hearing her that first time was a special moment for Samantha and me. We had just gotten back together after being broken up for ten months and were on the verge of starting a new chapter of our lives in Florida. Listening to Faydra play in that bar that night brought back memories of Samantha and me on Broadway when we met for the second time ever. Something sparked in us that night in 2016 and thanks to Faydra, it brought us closer again.

It's truly amazing how music can make such a big impact on someone's life. A melody sounds like a memory, and those memories bring out the best in us. Music can be therapeutic. While playing in a crowded bar, Faydra never knows who might walk in and be touched by her music. Those little moments of impacting people keep her moving forward in pursuing her dream of having her music played on the radio. Those moments make her realize that she is worthy and that pursuing her music career isn't a waste of time. She didn't have to become a doctor or lawyer to be important, like her high school teacher had suggested she do.

Living in Nashville and paying her bills by singing equates to success for Faydra. Another success for her is having someone pick up her own song, even if she's not playing it, and have it air on the radio for everyone to hear. While we were in Nashville, we filmed Faydra as she was recording her EP. Our favorite song on the EP is "Hey Tulsa!" Faydra is a true success in our minds. She is living out her dream of playing music as a full-time job. Music is all she has, which pushes her to go the extra mile.

She didn't let others sway her decision on her journey to Nashville, and even when getting started was tough, she kept pushing forward. When her teacher told her she was wasting her time, she ignored the advice and kept going with what she thought was right for her. As you go on your own journey to success, others will try to sway your decision and stop you from moving forward. Sometimes those people may even be the ones you look up to or love. Family could be trying to hold you back because, in their minds, they are giving you advice that they think is safe and right. Only you will know what's right for you and your dream.

Thinking Outside the Box for Sponsorships

As I have mentioned, of all the cities we visited, Nashville was our favorite. But it was also the city where we had to grind harder than ever to pull off the final episode *and* our wedding. As things drew closer, we began to realize how much everything was going to cost. My entrepreneur brain started to kick into high gear, and we started to think outside the box about how we would pull everything off.

Prior to filming in Nashville, Samantha had made a trip to a Taylor Swift concert in Kansas City with friends and from there a trip home to see her family. Each time Samantha left wherever we were living, I would go on nonstop working sprees. I slept very little and went into insane work mode. This time while she was gone, I told her that I would figure things out so we could pull off the last episode and our wedding day. That week, I probably sent more than 300 personalized emails to potential sponsors or client leads. I was looking for vendors to donate certain items for various parts of the wedding in return for exposure on our show and video clips they could use in their own marketing. I worked so hard to land a flower sponsor but had no luck. Now, every flower shop in Nashville knows who we are because of my emails! I didn't realize how expensive flowers were until we started getting quotes for them. Since we had no sponsors for the flowers, we ended up not having flowers. To be honest, no one realized it anyway.

I was also working to get a hotel sponsor to cover our film crew's stay while filming. I ended up walking into downtown hotels requesting to speak with managers. I would walk up to the front desk and with confidence say that I was filming a TV show in the city and putting on our wedding, which would be a part of the show. Each time, I would ask who I would need to talk to about sponsoring our program.

The front desk people were always impressed about the notion of the show, but once my request got to the manager or location decision maker, they usually shut me down. In one hotel, I waited for two hours in the lobby until the person came down to talk to me about being featured in a scene. Another hotel manager was very rude and didn't give me the time of day, even though I had waited for two hours. They couldn't care less about our wedding or that we were filming a show. To them, they saw no value in what we were offering, so I just moved on to the next place. After many people said no, I finally got a yes! Pine Street Flats, our apartment complex in Nashville, has a separate location that its management offered to our film crew to stay in during filming. It was a house that was ten minutes from our apartment. In return for this house, we created a promotional video of it for their marketing purposes. That was our first win that saved us money!

When we did film for the show, we used this house to put on a *Success in Your City* event. Through our connections in real estate from past cities and in Nashville, we sold tickets to a real estate video marketing and branding event. We also had help from our friend Brandon Green, who is well known in the Keller Williams real estate space. He helped us sell spots to the event and donated his time to speak at it. All event proceeds went toward film costs in Nashville. During the Nashville episode, we had to cut our film crew in half to save money. Samantha and I made sure to help where needed to fill in the gaps of having a smaller crew. Our crew got very little sleep while in Nashville because we crammed a lot of filming into a couple days.

The next sponsorship that we landed was our wedding venue, The Bell Tower. We researched all of the owners online and found that out one of them was a successful entrepreneur who had built the business from the ground up and owned multiple venues and a catering company. I had mad respect for what he had achieved. We reached out to him about featuring his venue in the show in return for sponsoring some of our wedding venue costs, and he agreed. We also created a video for the venue that included our wedding day, which resulted in an epic promotional video! After sending hundreds of emails, knocking on multiple doors in Nashville, trying to land bartering deals, and hearing many people say no, we had finally pulled everything all off. We funded the final episode of the show, and we had the wedding funded too!

The Wedding Day

Our wedding day was surreal. It's one of the most memorable parts of my life. Our friends and family were all there and also our film crew, who had become our family. In attendance were Shawn, Jeff, Kai, and Carlos, who had been our main film crew for the entire year. Mike, our business partner, was my groomsman, and Kevin Harrington, our executive producer, even took time out of his schedule to be there on our special day. Producers from past episodes and some of the featured stories of the show made it as well. James Whittaker, who was in the Austin episode, was the officiant and married us. Our wedding day was a finale of a show unlike any other.

Pulling off our wedding was probably the biggest obstacle that we overcame in 2018, given that we were planning a destination wedding while traveling the country, filming a TV show, and selling our house, all in the same year. Anyone who is planning a wedding will agree with me that it's a huge thing to pull off. Don't take my word for it, just ask Samantha, who planned most of it. Haha. But really, after looking back on it all, I wouldn't change a thing. Every obstacle we overcame made us who we are as a couple and brought us together stronger than ever.

While reading my vows to Samantha in front of everyone, it all became real for me. The woman I loved and had spent the past five years traveling with was about to become my wife. Before I let Samantha share her side of planning the entire wedding, I want to leave you with my vows that took me forever to write. After a music cowrite session with Faydra and her friends, and a little bit of inspiration from Google, I brought it all together.

My Vows to Samantha:

Samantha,

We have climbed many mountains together over the past five years. We have seen the ups and downs in business, life, and love. It hasn't always been easy, but it's been worth it.

Today I make my vow to you!

As your husband:

I will fight by your side until the day I die.

I will take care of you in sickness and in health.

I will strive to be the best me possible so I can be the best for you.

I will love you no matter what happens on this journey.

I will treat you the way you deserve to be treated as a woman.

I will have your back in any battle.

I will love you forever.

I've been successful with and without you by my side, but it's not truly success unless I have you! I want to achieve more, so I can be more for you. Through highways and hotels and sleeping on couches, I promise to always be the best me, to be the best for you.

Samantha, you are my success, my love, and my best friend for life.

I'm all yours, baby!

Chapter 12

Samantha

The Wedding in Nashville

Why We Chose Nashville

Nashville has a special place in my heart. Brandon and I spent one of our first weekends together there, and it is where I realized that nice men do exist. Like, "open your door for you nice." He took me out into the city, and we talked about life. We talked about how I was still struggling with letting go of the relationship I was in for eight years, and he talked about how he was overwhelmed by eighty-hour work weeks. Our lives were so similar, and I truly think we were attracted to each other to help each other move forward. I had never been to Nashville, and walking down Broadway was surreal. Live music and hundreds of people walking down the street surrounded us. Bars and rooftops were endless, and we danced and sang our little hearts out.

It was only our second time ever seeing each other, but I felt like I had known him for a lifetime. Since that first trip to Nashville, we have made it back there every year to relive that weekend that meant so much to both of us. When he proposed to me on October 13, 2017, I knew that Nashville would be where we would get married. I wanted to continue to have that city be a part of who we are.

Nashville was set to be the finale of the show. We wanted to feature a musician and highlight our wedding. After arriving in the city, we immediately looked at apartments to see if they offered short-term stays. As much as I disliked this process, we had to go through it to get a place where I would feel be comfortable. We had the wedding to finalize and the last episode to film, so my brain was scattered. Brandon made finding a place a priority to minimize us fighting about it.

With Nashville being our final city, we were getting pretty good at knowing how things worked, so we were able to find a place right away. We ended up going with Pine Street Flats, which was an apartment in the Gulch, and I loved the area as it was full of shops and restaurants. The energy in this part of town was so upbeat, and I was ready to start the long list that we needed to check off to make the wedding look somewhat together. I say that with seriousness, as anyone who has planned a wedding knows it takes so much thinking to make sure everything is ready for literally eight hours of fun.

On top of thinking about the wedding, we had someone special in mind to feature in this city. In 2016, we had stopped in Nashville while moving to Orlando, and our first stop was Margaritaville. We heard this powerful voice from the streets, and since I was searching for a female singer, I immediately cued Brandon to go in. That night, we sat at the bar and ordered drinks and an appetizer. The woman's voice so blew us away, we were almost in tears. Or at least I was. My friends tell me that I cry too much. Truth is, every emotion makes me cry. The singer's voice was beautiful, and she was playing so many of my favorite songs. I don't even think Brandon and I had a conversation. We just listened and appreciated what was right in front of us.

We wound up listening to her all night. Something about her was so special, and we continued to follow and listen to her on her Facebook Live videos over the next few years.

Being the crazy people we are, we messaged Faydra via Instagram and asked her when she would be playing next. She messaged back saying she would be at Margaritaville in a couple of days, and we were ecstatic. We wanted to ask her in person to be part of the show, so this was perfect. The only thing is that we had never talked to her in person before and she had no idea who we were. Hoping to catch her on a break, we went to see her play and sat at the same spot we saw her play the first time. After a few songs, she pointed at me and said, "Hey, aren't you the girl who messaged me on Instagram?" I was like, "YES, THAT WAS ME." Haha. I don't think I shouted it, but I became superexcited. On her break, the singer came over and we asked her if we could take her out to dinner to talk about why we were in town. She was so sweet and agreed to meet us the next week at our soon-to-be-favorite place to eat in the whole world, Bartaco. We were a step closer to finding our featured musician, and it excited me that it might be Faydra!

When Brandon and I brainstormed back at the apartment, we would talk about how much we needed to do for the wedding and for filming. We would just laugh and laugh and laugh and question each other about how the heck we had even arrived at this point without hurting each other. Seriously, the number of death stares we traded were endless the last nine months, and I praise us for not letting each other give up. We were both close, more me than him, and as much as it hurt at times and as broke as we were, we were still moving forward, and the wedding was still going to happen. I only called it off like seven times. Doesn't every soon-to-be wife? Haha.

We met Faydra at Bartaco. As we drove through the city, we reminisced about all of our memories there. We were excited to finally really talk to Faydra, who we had looked up to for years now. We were also hoping she would want to be a part of the TV show as we believed in her talent. I love Faydra for introducing us to this restaurant. On top of our great conversation, we had the most amazing tacos ever. They are life-changing tacos! You all know how much I love my food. We shared our mission with Faydra, and she was superinterested in it, which made me so happy. She was so perfect to feature because she truly was living her version of success. So when she said she wanted to join us on the show, I was thrilled. I can't imagine how she felt as some strangers rolled into town and asked her to be a part of their dream project. Good thing she was down to earth and didn't question if we were crazy. After dinner, we hugged and told her we would email her all of the details.

Planning the Wedding and Filming

So many things came back to haunt me when it was time to set up a wedding budget. I didn't want to put us in a situation where we spent everything we had on the wedding, but with it being a destination wedding, we were racking up quite the bill. I would eliminate things, but then we had to add things. It just continued to work that way until we just accepted the budget and worked hard to accomplish what we needed to do. Anyone who has planned a wedding knows the struggle. You want it to be "perfect," and I honestly didn't put into perspective how much even the littlest of things would cost.

Meanwhile, Brandon didn't have a desire to help with the wedding, so I was feeling so alone on top of stressing over money. Anytime I would ask him for advice, he said he didn't care, which resulted in me getting mad. This was *our* wedding, and he was so focused on the show. Didn't he know not to make the bride mad while planning a day that was for both of us? I should've just decorated it with unicorns and rainbows and called it a day. Haha. I ended up doing a lot of the wedding planning on my own, with a lot of help from my mom. She was there for anything I needed, and I'm so grateful she found the time, even 800 miles away.

Between the craziness, I had a previous trip planned to see Taylor Swift in Kansas City. I was stoked for this as I'm a huge fan. That girl speaks to my heart. I drove to KC from Nashville, which was a big deal for me. I never drove unless I had to. Brandon had driven from city to city the entire year, so I was happy when I arrived at the hotel safely. It felt good to just hang out with my friends and live like a normal person for the weekend. I say "normal" because with the show going on all year, I was so out of my element. It took a lot of energy and time to produce the show, which my body wasn't used to. KC was a much-needed getaway.

Two weeks before my KC trip, my nephew was born in Minnesota. So after KC, I was planning on driving to Minnesota to surprise some of my family. As I drove through Iowa, I couldn't help but smile because I was going to finally hug that little bundle of joy. Traveling and not being able to be there for his birth had been hard on me. My family is the most important thing in the world to me, and I felt guilt when I was unable to fly home. After I arrived in Minnesota, I made up for not seeing his first breath, but that is the kind of thing you have to deal with when you choose to be across the country. My nephew was so perfect, and I was so happy to be home for a couple of days. My mom and I got some of the decorations made, and we hung out eating our favorite pizza. It was hard to leave because I had no worries when I was home. I just got to relax, and my mind wasn't splattered all over the place.

When I arrived back in Nashville, I had so much on my mind. I feel like all of August and September was me just telling myself I had a full plate. I still had so much to do for the wedding. Like, pretty much everything. I was running in circles trying to get things done. On top of that, we still had to fly our crew in and find them a place to stay, which was getting so expensive and I had no idea how we were even going to pay for the wedding let alone the show. Between our two bank accounts, we didn't have enough money. This created a lot of tension between Brandon and me. This was testing us. Why on earth I planned a wedding the same year as traveling the country, I will never know. Brandon and I always make things work, but this wasn't easy. A lot of times, people thought we had it made, but in reality, we struggled deeply when it came to funding the show and funding our lives. We believed in the show, and when you have that much belief in something, you do whatever it takes to accomplish it—even if your happiness suffers momentarily.

As much as I wanted to do it, canceling the show was never an option. We did what had to be done, even if that was having a smaller crew come in. I was happy to have the guys in town for film week. Focusing on them and Faydra helped me stay away from overplanning the wedding. Sure, I was exhausted, but being around them made everything seem not so crazy. The focus was on Faydra and her story, and I literally could have listened to her sing all day. There is just something about her aura that attracts so much positive energy. We spent the week hearing her ups and downs on moving to Nashville. She had been through so much to get where she is today. We got to go to her studio, where she sang some of her songs off her EP. I was honored to even be in that room. Her passion for singing comes out in her voice. I had never experienced being in a studio with such a talented person. I left feeling inspired.

After filming was over, I recognized that we had accomplished a lot in just a few days; like hours and hours of filming and displaying a lot of dedication to get the right storyline so that we could impact others. It was overwhelming for everyone, but at the end of the day, we were always happy with the content. Faydra was so open to sharing her story and her music, and I was so grateful that she was a part of it. That girl is pure talent with the biggest heart. I loved hearing about her experience and how she chose to move to Nashville and pursue her dreams despite her favorite teacher telling her that she was making a mistake. And on top of spending the week with her, she agreed to play at our cocktail hour for the wedding, which was a dream come true.

The Wedding Is Here

I would be lying if I said funding the wedding was easy. We had help from my parents as well as Brandon's, and we still needed to come up with a big chunk of cash. We didn't expect the wedding to cost as much as it did, but I don't think any couple does. Our entire year of traveling and filming the show was way over budget, and we had to pay for things as they came. The wedding had to be paid for or there wouldn't be one. Talk about stress. We put every last penny into the wedding and didn't look back. I wish we had chosen to put on a smaller wedding in my hometown to save money, but I knew our overall experience would be something I would never forget.

I had ordered my wedding dress back in May on rush shipping and was getting nervous as I still hadn't received it in mid-September. Our wedding was October 13, and I was freaking out! I called the bridal shop, and someone there informed me that the dress would arrive in the next couple of days. Luckily, they were right. But with my dress in hand, I realized it needed to be altered. Suddenly, I was calling around to see if I could get in to see someone with a two-week deadline. I had no idea how much time altering takes, but I was lucky enough to find Karen Hendrix Couture online. She was able to get me in last minute. Thank you, Karen! After she finished her alterations, I modeled my dress for her and I was surprised to find that it fit perfectly. I'd had nightmares that it was going to be too small.

Well, the dress sparkled so beautifully, and I couldn't believe I was getting married. *Where has the time gone?* I wondered. *Do I still have time to run?* Haha, I'm only kidding; but after the year Brandon and I had been though, I was surprised that the wedding was still on. I mean, can you blame me? Brandon had tested me to the max. Now, since the dress fit, all we needed to do was put some hooks on it so I could dance at the reception. I had no idea what that meant, but I know Karen did, so I agreed and was told the dress would be ready in a couple of weeks. I was happy to check that off the list.

My brain was stirring at the number of things I had left to do. Who would have thought that so much detail went into one night? One night! I mean seriously. Decorations. Food. Dessert. Music. Napkins. Chairs. The list is endless. Good thing Brandon was so much help. Not. He didn't help at all. I guess I was happy to be in charge of what the night would look like, but of course, I gave Brandon crap for not helping because that is what overwhelmed fiancées do. Right? He had no interest in helping as he was focused on the show, so I had to take the lead in tackling the to-do list so our wedding looked somewhat put together. Overall, I enjoyed finding the decor and searching for the best cupcakes because I love planning parties, but I did miss the fact that my mom couldn't physically be there to help me with the arrangements. Thankfully, she was superhelpful via phone, and I don't think I could have pulled off what we did without her. Nope, there wouldn't have been a wedding without her.

I was anxious as my parents drove to Nashville from Minnesota, a twelve-hour drive. They had my niece and two-month-old nephew with them. I was hoping to help them with the drive, but I just had way too much to do so I couldn't fly to Minnesota and then drive back to Nashville with them. I was happy to see them when they finally arrived. Being away from them all year was hard. I loved that they got to get out of Minnesota and explore Nashville a little bit. We were planning on having the wedding party and both of our families over for Nashville's famous chicken from Hattie B's. We all met in the outside gardens of the apartment where we were staying. Having everyone together was nice, and I loved that we could socialize a bit to make the actual wedding day more comfortable. No one wants to go into a big event where no one knows anyone. It was a really good time, and I felt much better going into the wedding the following day.

Brandon had decided he was going to stay in a hotel the night before the wedding and I would stay at our apartment with my best friend, Megan. I had to finish up the seating chart, which never got done. Oops. You can't make everything perfect. I had my sisters over as well, and we made sure all the decorations were packed up to bring to the venue the next day. Megan and I also loaded up on tacos from Bartaco. She had never had them and I was craving them, so we ran and picked some up. So good. We sat up and talked about life per usual and just couldn't believe the wedding was the next day. Time flew, and I felt I did the best I could with the limited resources we had. Every bride wishes she could have done more and then when it's all done and over, we think that we should have done less. Well, that's my personal opinion anyway.

Our wedding day was here, and I woke up to my favorite coffee from my sister Aubrey and a gift from Brandon. He had made me a journal of our lives together so far. Ironically, my gift to him was the same. He had filled his gift to me with pictures and his favorite memories of us. I could tell he had spent a lot of time on that journal, and so now it all made sense why he hadn't had time to plan the wedding. Haha! Kidding, but not really. He brought up so many good memories about how much we had done together in the short five years we had been a couple. He also gave me a Tiffany ring and necklace that said, "LOVE." I had wanted that set for a while, and I couldn't imagine a more perfect day to receive it from him. I might have cried a little bit. Just a little bit.

We had planned on meeting the rest of the wedding party at the venue where we were going to get ready for the service. I was in charge of the ladies, and Brandon was in charge of the guys. I prayed that his half of the wedding party would show up. I mean, can you blame me? His head was consumed by all of his work, and I don't even know if he would have known there was a wedding if I didn't remind him. Okay, maybe I'm exaggerating, but there is a little truth in that. As I arrived at the venue, we all hung up our dresses and showed each other how we wanted our hair and makeup. Decisions, I tell you. I left it up to everyone to do whatever they wanted. I didn't want everyone to look the same. I feel that everyone has their own style. I had already known what I wanted, so that was one less thing to think about. We spent around four hours getting ready and singing our hearts out while in preparation for the ceremony. Yes, four hours. I had a pretty big wedding party, so they took a tad bit longer than the boys. The boys had it easy!

Then came the pictures. Oh my goodness, did this part make me anxious. Getting everyone together and looking at the camera all together was hard. It didn't help that everyone was hungry. I was hungry too, but I needed these pictures to be perfect! I know that perfect doesn't exist but as the bride you just want the day to go as smoothly as possible. Thank goodness we had amazing photographers who had been traveling with us all year. Kai and Jeff were there to capture the day, and I was so thankful for them. Shawn also helped, and I loved that because he knows exactly what I like and don't like. Heck, he even knows what my better side is when it comes to pictures. They were so calm in the midst of me being a little brat. I just wanted the pictures to be something I would treasure forever. And guess what? They turned out great just as I was promised. Thanks, guys!

My dad was so nervous to walk me down the aisle because he didn't want to step on my dress. So, of course, I kept giving him crap that he had better keep his shoes off my white dress, which probably made him more nervous. But what else are daughters for? As we were about to walk down the aisle, I felt so scared. Scared on my wedding day? Who was I? It was just finally hitting me that I was about to be married. MARRIED. Not in a million years did I think I was going to find a man that I loved so much I would marry him. I know that Brandon and I loved each other, but the stress we had endured over the year almost made us break up several times.

As I prepared to marry Brandon, I wondered, *Will I always have that resentment toward him? Will we meet in the middle when it comes to some things?* I had no idea that these thoughts would overcome me five minutes before walking down the aisle, but they did. It's not like I wanted to run away, but I was a little worried. Every bride overanalyzes this as it's a huge commitment to read your vows in front of everyone, and you have to be sure that this is what you want. I know it is what I wanted, but the challenges Brandon and I had endured just months before were always on my mind. We had gotten through them, so I know we had the heart to get through anything else together—even if that means putting him in his place. Haha.

Walking down the aisle was surreal. Brandon looked so handsome, and to have everyone close to us there witness us show our love to each other was amazing. A close friend, James, married us, and he did such a great job. He was great at storytelling, and it wasn't like any other ceremony I had been to. Brandon and I read each other our vows, and tears were shed. I didn't think I would be that nervous but dang is it hard with all eyes on you. I forgot some of my words and nearly blacked out, but overall, I think we did pretty well up there.

We started out the night with cocktail hour, which consisted of hors d'oeuvres and an open bar. Oh, what an idea an open bar was. I laugh so hard still at some of the video footage from the night. Perhaps

I may never show it, but there is always that small chance. We were lucky enough to get Faydra to play during happy hour. It was a magical moment. She played her song "Hey Tulsa!" and I about lost it. I was like that fangirl at a concert. I just have so much love for her, and she inspires me to continue doing whatever it is that makes me happy. Everyone loved the live music, and it was great to see everyone in one room mingling and enjoying the conversation.

Our ceremony was in the same building as our reception, so as we had cocktail hour on the patio, they were setting up tables inside for us to have dinner. I can't even tell you if the right people were sitting next to each other because as a bride, I think on the day of the wedding you just give up on half the tasks that truly don't even matter. I just wanted to enjoy the moments and hang out with everyone who flew in to be with us on our special day. All I know was that there was food on the tables and drinks in everyone's hands. People were laughing and dancing, and the room was beautiful. Everything was coming together in a way that I had once envisioned.

Okay, so onto speeches. The moment my sister—who was my matron of honor—stood up, I knew something crazy was going to happen. She had a suspicious expression, which made me think, *What is she going to do?* She was always the fun party girl in the group, but what she presented next was something I didn't expect. She cued the DJ to turn the music on, and I was shaking. Of all things, an Eminem song came on and my sister started rapping. I about dropped! We all were laughing so hard, and I think she had a little too many drinks. Regardless, she owned that moment. Never in a million years did I think she would make a rap about Brandon and me, and then rap it in front of that many people. I was literally in tears from shock and laughing so hard. Best speech ever! And maybe even best sister award ever as well.

Brandon and I had a tough time choosing our first dance song. It is *so* hard to just choose one song that will be a reminder of such a special moment. So, since we couldn't decide on one together, I just made the choice. Haha. Winning. I mean, I planned the entire wedding anyway; I might as well have ended up the planning with a bang. I chose "Perfect" by Ed Sheeran because I liked these words, "I will not give you up this time." These lyrics resonated with me as Brandon and I, at one point, had broken up for ten months, and I honestly had not believed we would ever get back together. I mean just ask my friends. I was *never* getting back with him, and here I was a few years later, married to him. But I just love that Sheeran song and found it perfect for us. Dancing with my husband for the first time was magical. I was filled with so much love, and I couldn't believe that we had made it this far. It was an obstacle, but I was thanking God that I was matched with such a man as Brandon T. Adams.

The rest of the night consisted of a lot of dancing, great conversation, and a whiskey tasting. The whiskey room was so beautiful, stunning. It was an add-on that didn't come with the venue cost, but I thought that the experience would be great for the guests. The walls were lined with hundreds of whiskeys, and above hung the original bell from the church. The venue was originally a church that had been renovated into an event space, so it was very historic, which I loved. The history is one of the reasons I chose to get married at The Bell Tower. At one point in the night, we did the dollar dance and *I lost*. Brandon made more money than I did, and I wasn't surprised, but come on. The bride always wins. Brandon probably paid someone to put in a big amount so he could win. Haha. Kidding.

But I was disappointed because I had thought that for sure I would win the dollar dance. Meanwhile, I loved dancing with each guest individually who participated. It gave me time to express how thankful I was for their presence and to talk to them a little bit. We ended the night with lining everyone up and lighting sparklers. I had seen amazing shots of brides and grooms walking by sparklers, and I wanted to do the same. As we did, our photographer got jabbed with one and it burned his head. My friend almost lit my hair on fire! I wish I were kidding. I guess an open bar for five hours plus fire don't mix. Who would have thought! Overall, the night was so beautiful, and I was so grateful for our parents, who helped us pull it off.

One thing I wish could have been different: that we had been able to talk to every one of our 130 guests. When they say that you don't talk to everyone at your wedding, they are not lying. It was a challenge. I was just enjoying myself after all the stress it took to even have the wedding happen. I was happy to hear that everyone loved the flow of the entire wedding. All I know is that I'm so happy that I will only be getting married once. It's expensive, and you stress way too much for what is only an eight-hour event. Why do we do this to ourselves? Well, I wouldn't change the outcome, but I now understand the advice I got from brides who said, "Don't sweat the small stuff." This is easier said than done, but it's so true. It's one day, and most likely it will go so fast that all of the stuff you wish you had done doesn't even matter. Just remember that it is a day that celebrates the love between two people and that a flower wall or fancy chairs will not define the amount of love that you have for each other.

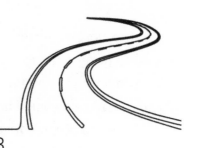

Chapter 13
Brandon

Life after the Show

O ur wedding was one of the best experiences of our lives and was the ultimate finale of our year together and the TV show. We had just completed our commitment for 2018 to travel the country, film the show, and have our wedding. The fact that we had pulled it all off blew our minds.

The morning after the wedding, we were still in shock. We felt free and at peace knowing we were married, the wedding had happened as planned, and that we no longer had to think about the next city to travel to or the next episode to film, at least for season one. For once in ten months, we could rest and put our minds at ease.

On our first full day as newlyweds, we went to breakfast with my parents and then met up with some other family and friends who had made the trip to be with us on our special day. We spent the next few days in Nashville having time for ourselves and doing fun things. We went on some dinner dates at our favorite restaurants, checked out some bars on Broadway, and spent private time together. Originally, we had planned to do our dream honeymoon right away in Hawaii, but we wanted to delay our trip. Filming the final episode for our show and putting on a wedding in the same thirty-day period was not cheap! We settled on having a mini honeymoon in Vail, Colorado. While filming in Denver, we had become friends with a family who appeared in a scene of our show and they had offered us time in their condo in Vail for free as a wedding gift. Just six days after we had wed, we were in Vail enjoying time together. In forty-eight hours, we had driven from Nashville to Garnavillo to Des Moines to Vail—not for the show, but for us.

During our three days in Vail, we dined at restaurants, toured the city, and drove into the mountains in our Tahoe. We almost got stuck in the snow, but with my great driving skills we managed to avoid that. During this time, we got back in touch with ourselves and, for the first time in a year, our conversations weren't tied around the show. The show had become our identity, which sometimes took away our ability to just be a couple in a relationship, not a couple who are TV hosts. This happens to many couples who go into business together: They become tied to their business and so involved with it as a team that they forget to switch off business mode and turn on relationship mode. Samantha was always the one to let me know when I needed to stop being the business partner/ TV host and be her fiancé. My mind is always going, and it's not always easy to just shut it off and not think about my goals for the show. I've always been that way. I think it's a disease that all entrepreneurs suffer from. We always want to think about our next move, our next strategy.

After three amazing days in Vail, we made our way toward Minneapolis, where we planned to settle down in an apartment for at least a year. Samantha wanted to live in Minnesota so she could be close to her family, who live in the state. She wanted to make up for the time she didn't get to see them in the previous years. After all our travels and everything I put her through, I was going to give her whatever she wanted, even if that meant living in Minnesota for a year. I just needed to be close to an airport so I could easily fly to different cities for speaking engagements. Being in Minneapolis also meant I was only a four-hour drive from my family in Iowa.

We were confident we would find an apartment right away on day one. Samantha had already picked three places to look at. But ultimately, none of them were the right fit for us. We ended up spending three days looking for a place and didn't find our home until the fifteenth apartment tour! We settled on a beautiful place in downtown Minneapolis; it had a great view of the city and was right by the new football stadium. Samantha is a big Vikings fan, so it worked out! After picking our new home, we made our way back to Iowa to grab stuff from our storage unit in Garnavillo. Within a few days, we were back in Minneapolis and moved into our apartment. Having a home base felt good. It also made me happy knowing that Samantha was happy. She had been wanting to have a place to call home for a long time.

When you go from city to city sleeping in different hotels and apartments, you forget what it feels like to have a place that is truly yours. There is something incredibly calming about having your own home. In just ten months, we had been in more than forty states in the US and in well over 100 cities. In less than one year, we had put on over 50,000 miles on our Tahoe. We had taken our travel life to an entirely new level; it now felt good to have down time in one place.

We officially moved into our apartment in Minneapolis on October 27, just two weeks after our wedding. Now that we were settled, we started to think about what was next for *Success in Your City* and for our own personal endeavors. We had to think about how we were going to make money again as entrepreneurs and what areas we would focus on. While filming the show and traveling, we had put a lot of things on hold. Samantha wasn't training fitness clients, and I had basically put the brakes on Accelerant Media Group for a while. I wasn't running campaigns for clients but had a few advisory roles that paid me. I wanted to put all of my focus on getting our show picked up by a network and landing a distribution deal that would pay us to license our content. We had invested close to $250,000 into the show and hadn't paid ourselves yet. We also had two years of sweat equity built up in creating the *Success in Your City* show and brand.

Since getting a licensing deal was more of a long-term play, we needed to figure out ways to make money so we could pay our bills and live. During this time, I was still trying to sell Adams' Ice Service. It had been taking longer than expected to get an offer for it, and the process was starting to drain me. It took a lot of time and energy to provide all the necessary content for the interested buyer and the sale kept getting delayed.

I was focusing on three main areas now: landing a distribution deal for the show, selling the ice business, and building up a revenue stream to live off of. Again, I wanted all my focus to be on the show, but the other two areas needed attention no matter what. When I thought about making money, all I could think of was making it so I could put it right back into the show. I didn't need any material things, and I hated spending money on anything that wasn't an investment in the show or our future. Samantha will be the first to tell you that I'm really cheap at times and hate spending money on nonsense things. As long as I have food to survive, I'm good to go. Now, when it came to the show, I would spend every penny we had toward making it the best show possible and creating a platform that positively impacts the world. I believe all entrepreneurs can relate with me in some way here.

Entrepreneurs want to grow their business and idea and have it do big things. It's their baby. They will do whatever it takes to make it go and will make many sacrifices along the way. The entrepreneurs who never quit and make the biggest sacrifices are the ones who eventually turn their company or idea into a major success. Many people will never understand that about entrepreneurs. We are just wired differently and think in a totally different way. Even Samantha couldn't quite grasp why and how I did the things that I did for my entrepreneurial endeavors and the lengths I went through for our show.

When I commit to something, I give it everything I've got. I go all in. I had set out to do that when we first had the idea and mission for *Success in Your City*. I was in for the long haul and had mentally prepared myself for what was ahead. That's why it was difficult for me when I couldn't just focus solely on the show. I also had to focus on selling the ice business while trying to generate revenue to provide for Samantha and me. I didn't want to get our marriage off on the wrong foot; it was my duty to take care of the woman I loved.

Over the next few months, we were getting back into a routine and collaborating on ideas for the show and for making money to survive. Samantha struggled with figuring out what she wanted to do while I struggled with how I could find ways to make money *while* doing the show. Making money wasn't exactly hard for me, but making sure that how I made it aligned with our mission for the show was difficult. I no longer wanted to do video shoots for other companies for extra income. If I was going to do a video shoot, I wanted it to be for *Success in Your City*. It became clear to me that coaching or consulting and speaking gigs would help me earn some additional money and allow me to remain focused on the show.

I would find that coaching entrepreneurs or consulting for companies only took a few hours per week and that speaking at events led to me sharing our vision of the show while also finding clients in the crowds. Within one week of moving into our place in Minneapolis, I was already on a plane to speak at an event in Los Angeles. I was determined to spread our mission as soon as possible to any crowd I could get in front of.

Working toward a distribution deal for *Success in Your City* consisted of having many meetings with people in the industry who had either sold shows or had connections to individuals at various networks. Everyone loved the show concept, and everyone also provided feedback about what we should do differently. We spoke with many production companies that had recognition in Hollywood and the capability to pitch to networks like Netflix, Amazon, Hulu, ABC, NBC, and more. Some companies had an interest in pitching the show, but they wanted to change it around and use what we had filmed as a pitch deck in hopes of landing a distribution deal. That might require us to then go and reshoot the show and make changes to the original concept. That was not an option for us.

Some companies wanted to make the focus more about us and not so much about the success stories we had featured. Some people told us we should sell our concept to a network and let them reshoot our show with a known celebrity. We were told we weren't famous enough and that networks didn't like buying shows unless a well-known host was already established as part of the show. I get that we weren't known as TV stars like Chip and Joanna Gaines, but we were working toward that. Once, no one knew Chip and Joanna either.

Hearing all of this kind of feedback began to frustrate us. Everyone always said our show had amazing cinematography and editing and that they loved Samantha and me as the hosts . . . but there was always something they wanted to change. Samantha and I knew we had a great show, and we weren't about to give in by selling ourselves short and doing what others thought we should. That didn't align with our own success and what we believed the success of the show should be.

While talking with TV show rep companies and production companies, we were also sending emails to executives at major networks. We were sending them show clips and sharing our mission with them. This is isn't industry standard—not how things are done in Hollywood—but everything we had done for *Success in Your City* wasn't industry standard or "how things are done" in the industry. Normally, selling a show to a network goes like this: A production company shoots a pilot and then pitches the show concept to a network. This production company usually has had experience selling shows to networks or has a major celebrity or executive producer tied to the show, or what we would call a "showrunner." Because of the name recognition of the EP or showrunner, or a past connection with the network, the production company can get in the door to pitch their show concept. They then pitch the show concept to the network. If the network likes it, they will pay a lump sum for X number of episodes of the show and the production company will use that money to produce the show and provide it for the network to air on their platform. In most cases, TV show pilots are shot and are never picked up by a network.

The obstacle with our show: A known production company did not create *Success in Your City*, and we didn't have a showrunner known in Hollywood. The production companies we talked to had the connections and ability to pitch the show to our desired networks, but they would only do that if we changed our show around. That wasn't an option for us. Some companies didn't like that we had filmed the entire season already; by doing that, they automatically had no creative control over the content and couldn't fully put their name on it as the creators of the work. There is a lot of ego involved in this industry, if you ask me. Because of these reasons, we couldn't even get the meetings with the networks because we couldn't find a production company that truly saw our vision and was willing to pitch our show the way we wanted it to be pitched.

These were the exact reasons why we started directly emailing the networks ourselves. We knew there was a small chance they would take us seriously, but that small chance was the only option we felt we had. We did research online and found the email addresses for the executives and TV show buyers for all the networks we were interested in. Almost none of them responded to our emails, but they did open them. Since we have HubSpot, we were able to track the exact time they had opened the mail. I personally sent twelve emails to an executive at Netflix, though he did not respond to any of them. I believe persistence is key. We had nothing to lose. We wanted to let them know we were serious.

We extensively researched each executive. In emails, we let them know that by mentioning things about them that we had in common, like growing up in the same state, having mutual friends in the industry, or liking a similar sport. To give you an idea of what these emails look like, I will list them for you. To keep the people's names at these companies private, we will call them "Joe" instead of using their real names.

Email to executive at Hulu before we won Emmy Awards:

Hey Joe,

Congrats on your TV career. It's pretty impressive what you have accomplished over the years.

With your extensive experience from FOX Sports, I'm guessing you have come across Shea Hillenbrand, who played for the Boston Red Sox and LA Dodgers. Shea is in an episode of our show.

I'm reaching out to have a conversation about having our TV series Success in Your City on Hulu.

We have already filmed Season 1 of the show and are in post-production. The show will be ready to release in 2019.

Based off of Hulu's core audience being millennials and people who have an interest in travel, I feel this original series would be a perfect match for Hulu.

My wife and I have traveled the country this year living in different cities across the US on a mission to redefine the meaning of success through amazing stories from [people of] various backgrounds and experiences.

We featured stories in these cities:

1. *Scottsdale, AZ*
2. *Austin, TX*
3. *Boston, MA*
4. *Denver, CO*
5. *Nashville, TN*

You can watch our trailer of the show at SuccessinYourCity.com/ RedefineSuccess

Here is an intro to the Scottsdale episode with Shea Hillenbrand: https://youtu.be/6PGsdOsuh9o

We have an Emmy Award winning team, a 5X Emmy Award winning director and our executive producers are Kevin Harrington "Original Shark from Hit Show Shark Tank" and Jeff Hoffman "Co-founder of Priceline.com." Recently we received two Emmy nominations. One for the trailer of the show and one for the Shea Hillenbrand Story.

At your convenience, we are available to do a call or meeting in person with you to go over the show in depth and share the vision of future seasons of Success in Your City.

Your time is much appreciated!

Sincerely,

Brandon T. Adams

P.S. Here is a photo of my wife and I on set in Austin, TX.

(Picture was inserted)

Email to executive at Amazon Studios after we won Emmy Awards:

Hey Joe,

Congratulations on your amazing track record in such a short period of time! I saw your past jobs on LinkedIn.

I can only imagine how great your current job is at Amazon Studios. Amazon has come out with some pretty epic content over the past few years for movies and shows.

I'm fairly new to the TV industry but like you, in a short period of time I've been able to gain some experience through the movie Think and Grow Rich: The Legacy and the TV show Ambitious Adventures.

My wife and I spent all of 2018 traveling the country and filming our own series called Success in Your City.

You can watch our show trailer at SuccessinYourCity.com/Redefine-Success

We have already filmed season 1 of the show.

Our trailer recently won an Emmy Award and we also won an Emmy for a mini-doc we produced featuring Shea Hillenbrand.

We have considered Amazon as a home for our show.

Would you be able to help direct me to who I should be talking to at Amazon for our show? Or maybe I should be having a conversation with you?

I appreciate your time and help.

Sincerely,

Brandon T. Adams

We also emailed Netflix, but I will save that email for later in the book when I talk about our Netflix journey.

Preparing just one email for an executive took hours. Each had to be personal and stand out. We put in the time and research to learn about these individuals so that our message didn't sound like another spam email that was sent to everyone else. It was very frustrating spending all this time on the emails and sending them only to find out that the people on the other end would open them but never reply, even after as much as a dozen reach outs. Some may call it crazy, some may call it annoying, and some may call it stalkerish, but I call it the persistence necessary to get a point across.

Persistence is key to any success. Some of the greatest actors in Hollywood got turned down hundreds of times before they got their foot in the door. They always showed up and kept striving to prove themselves and their worth to get the role. That's exactly what we were doing. Every major actor or TV producer was once a beginner and a no-name who kept showing up until someone gave them a chance. We kept showing up in the network's inboxes waiting for one of them to give us our chance. It just takes one person to change your life. We were determined to find that person!

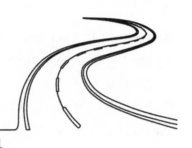

Chapter 14
Brandon

The Road to the Emmys

If you had asked me five years ago what an Emmy Award is or what it stands for, I wouldn't have known what to say. In fact, Samantha and I had no clue what Emmys were until I got involved with the show *Ambitious Adventures*. As a kid, I had always watched the awards that were given to actors and TV producers for their work, but I never knew what they really meant. It seemed like something that would be impossible for a kid from a small town in Iowa to achieve. It was foreign to me.

I will never forget the night Greg Rollett called me to say that the Hollywood episode of *Ambitious Adventures* was nominated for an Emmy. At the time, Samantha and I were in Santa Monica, California, during our mini-tour for *Success in Your City*. As soon as I found out about the nomination, I called my dad and said, "Dad, I'm nominated for an Emmy Award!" "What's an Emmy?" he asked. My brother and sister didn't even believe me when I first told them about the nomination. My brother actually had to look it up online and see the proof on the website. Then he posted it on Facebook to let others know what his younger brother had been nominated for. It was a proud moment for me because very rarely did my brother acknowledge my accomplishments publicly.

Fast forward six weeks later, and it was December 2, 2017. Samantha, me, and the rest of the *Ambitious Adventures* team that had spent the past eighteen months putting their hearts and souls into the show were at the Suncoast Emmy Awards ceremony in Orlando. Samantha was excited and nervous for me because she knew how hard I had worked on the show. She had even watched me film a few of the episodes. Suddenly, we were just moments away from the category that *Ambitious Adventures* had been nominated in. We were about to find out if we were going to take home Emmy Awards or go home emptyhanded. As the presenters announced our category, my heart started racing and I began to shake. In a matter of seconds, however, I went from excitement and nervousness to disappointment and defeat. Our names weren't announced. We would be going home without the prize.

Greg and I both felt defeated. I didn't understand why we hadn't won because the show was shot so well, and we had put everything we had into it. That moment made me realize that sometimes, even when you give something everything you've got, you still may fall short of your goal. That night, something happened to me that started a fire inside me. I had never been so motivated and determined in my life. That night, I told myself that I was going to work my butt off and do whatever it took to come back the following year to win an Emmy for *Success in Your City*.

I've always been competitive and a person who strives to do his best. I wanted to win an Emmy to prove to others that we have what it takes as TV producers and hosts to create something that reaches a high level of achievement. Maybe there was still a little of my younger child inside of me trying to prove my worth to others. Either way, I wanted to win, and I was going to put in the work to make that happen. I even named my phone alarm "Time to Grind, Emmy, Every Day." Every morning, it went off at five thirty. I was making sure to remind myself that I needed to put in the work every day when I woke up.

During the first six months of our *Success in Your City* tour, we filmed three episodes and also captured other content that could be used to make short documentaries on each person we featured. In June, we submitted our material in multiple categories to the Suncoast Regional Chapters. We submitted the documentary *The Shea Hillenbrand Story: Against All Odds*, and we submitted the trailer for *Success in Your City* in the promotional category under cinematography.

I've had my work judged before to be considered for an Emmy Award, and this year (2019) I've even been on the other side judging other projects that were up for Emmy consideration. I'm going to share with you some of the things I believe will make your work become powerful in a way to inspire others and be considered for winning an award.

Powerful stories can make a huge impact on our world, and using video to tell a story can spread it to the masses quickly. A story that inspires, motivates, and emotionally touches the viewer is what people want to see. After someone watches the story on video, they should feel something that makes them want to do more with their lives or the video should really hit home with them and their emotions. Great stories show moments of adversity and failure and how an individual or group overcame the obstacle and achieved the impossible. These success stories give viewers hope to achieve their own goals and go after their own dreams. This is a big reason why Samantha and I are so passionate about *Success in Your City* and sharing other stories with the world through our show.

The video content used for a story needs to be high quality and edited in a way that tells the story in the best way possible. You must have the right equipment, the right cinematographers, and the right editors. The majority of the content we filmed in 2018 was captured on several Cannon 200s, a top of the line camera that allows you to film in many formats and has many features that allow you to capture the best footage.

Even when you have the best equipment, you still need the best cinematographers with experience using the cameras and know-how to capture the best footage. To film *Success in Your City*, we partnered with our director, Shawn Vela. Shawn has been in this industry for more than a decade and has won thirteen Emmy Awards in his career to date. Shawn and his team captured the necessary content in each city to tell the most impactful stories.

The final piece of the puzzle is editing the video content. Editing will make or break the entire project. Shawn and assistant editor Carlos Medina have worked together to edit our show and also its trailer and the Shea Hillenbrand documentary. Editing consists of using the right footage, adding in meaningful special effects and pictures, and using the right kind of music to create necessary emotions for certain points in the video. Music is a big component that ties into the editing process. The next time you watch a movie or TV show, notice how much the music creates emotions for you.

The entire process of creating a powerful video is exhilarating. So many pieces make up the puzzle, and the best part as a producer is to see the final product come together and be released to the masses. When you see the emotions it creates for others and the positive impact it has on them, you feel fulfilled as a producer and content creator. You work so hard to get to the point where your work positively affects others, and when you do get there, that's when you see that your hard work has paid off. Now, when Samantha and I watch a TV show or movie, we look at it so differently. We respect the hard work put into it, and we think about how we can take ideas from what we're watching and apply it to our own work.

Personally, actors and filmmakers have always intrigued me because of their ability to motivate me and inspire me to go after all the things I do today in my life. I'm sure you have a favorite movie you've watched that you will never forget. What's the name of that movie? What about it inspired you, and what did it inspire you to do with your life? That inspiration is exactly why Samantha and I put our hearts and souls into *Success in Your City*—to create that same feeling to inspire you to go after your own success.

In October, the month we got married, we found out that we were nominated for two Emmy Awards—one for the Hillenbrand documentary and another for the TV show trailer. I will never forget Samantha waking me up late at night and saying, "Brandon, we are nominated!" We were one step closer to winning the award. Just two months later, we were at the same awards ceremony as the year before where I had so much fire inside me after not hearing my name called. Now, Samantha and I were so nervous and excited for our chance to win.

When our categories were announced, I prayed. Some people reading this may think I'm crazy or overthinking this whole award, but to me, Samantha, and everyone else involved with the show, it was more than an Emmy. We all had worked so hard to get to this point. Samantha and I had been through so much together. We had almost lost everything in the process. There weren't many people as committed as us to one project. We had sold our house, a business, given away most of our things, committed over a year of our lives to the show, and didn't get paid in the process. We put our entire lives into the show.

As we sat in the room with more than 1,000 other attendees and even more viewers from the livestream, we held our breaths as the hosts opened up the envelope to announce the winners. They opened their mouths, and the next words that came out never sounded so good. We won! We won Emmy Awards! In that moment, nothing else mattered. We had just shown everyone who believed in us and also didn't believe in us, that we had won. We showed everyone that we were capable of achieving such a noteworthy accomplishment. Our team ended up winning Emmy Awards for both Shea's story and the trailer. It was an amazing night that we will cherish forever.

To Samantha and me, winning the award was about more than the trophy. It was about showing others our dedication and commitment to one project. Everything we had done in our lives had led up to this point, a major milestone that we will never forget. We all have the chance to win our own Emmys in life. We all have the chance to achieve something of significance that shows others how hard we have worked toward a goal. To achieve any kind of significant success, you have to work for it. It won't come easy. Nothing worth achieving comes easy, and you wouldn't want it to. Work hard, stick with it, and don't quit until you achieve it!

Chapter 15
Brandon

The Netflix Journey

January had come and we still didn't have the meeting we wanted with one of our targeted networks. We also didn't have actual representation from a TV rep yet. We were frustrated and felt like we were making no progress. Originally, we had planned on releasing the show in February 2018, but with no network deal for additional funding to edit the show into final format, we had a ways to go. It felt as if no one cared about our show. Maybe they didn't. No one will ever care about your idea as much as you will, nor will they work as hard as you to make it a success. At the end of the day, you, the founder or creator, will be the one who puts in the necessary work and goes the extra mile to make it to the finish line.

After two months of no real progress, we had to do something different, otherwise we weren't going to get anywhere. I get that things take time, but sometimes you have to do something way out of the ordinary to switch things up. Netflix was the network that was number one on our list for hosting our show. We had been studying their platform and their core team that had created the empire. We were on a mission to show Netflix how our show was different than anything else and how we, the hosts and creators, were different.

Our strategy: send packages about our show directly to Netflix executives. I also planned to show up at their headquarters with the hopes of meeting with a higher-up executive or a person in the buying department for TV shows like ours. I also planned to document the entire journey with my GoPro and iPhone to publish it on social media. I wanted others to know how serious we were about landing a network deal.

When we told others about our idea, many thought we were crazy, and they were probably mostly right. Just showing up at Netflix headquarters and expecting a meeting is not something you do in the industry. They require a scheduled meeting by way of a legit TV representative. But as I mentioned before, we couldn't find the right representative that aligned with our goals and would pitch the show the way we wanted them to. Because of that, it felt like we had no option but to go straight to the source, even if we had a 1 percent chance of landing a meeting with a representative at Netflix. One percent is better than 0 percent. We had to give it a shot. I told Samantha that if I didn't show up at Netflix and at least try I would regret it for the rest of my life. I'd always wonder, *What if?* I don't ever want to be the "what if" person, and you shouldn't either. Living life with regrets is not a life to live.

One week before my trip to Netflix HQ, Samantha and I spent a few days creating custom packages for various members of the streaming service. We had done an insane amount of research on four specific individuals that worked there and thought they would be the ones that would give us the best chance of granting the meeting we desired for pitching our show. These packages included handwritten letters written to the individuals along with pictures from the set of the show and thumb drives that had each of their names on it. Each thumb drive had sizzle clips from our show, a pitch deck, and a custom video from Samantha and me speaking directly to the person. In the package, we also included a PR release mock-up that showed us on the cover of *The Hollywood Reporter* with the title "Netflix Redefines Success." Additionally, we presented an entire story that was written as if we had already partnered together. It was our way of standing out.

Here is the mock-up article, titled "Netflix Partners with Newlyweds to Redefine Success," that we sent to Netflix team members:

Netflix has started the New Year off with some BIG surprises and momentum, already releasing hit shows, such as Black Mirror's "Bandersnatch," Taylor Swift's "Reputation Stadium Tour," and the new movie, "Bird Box," featuring Sandra Bullock, which already has been watched by 45 million subscribers. Netflix recently announced their newest partnership which is unlike any they have made before and it's certain to open the eyes of viewers on the real truth of what success really is. Netflix just confirmed that this spring they will release the TV series "Success in Your City" with co-hosts and newlyweds Brandon T. Adams and Samantha Rossin, a couple from a small town in Iowa.

"Success in Your City" is a TV series that is on a mission to redefine the meaning of success and change the way that others view success. All throughout 2018, Brandon and Samantha lived in different cities across the country and experienced the daily lives of individuals who are living their own unique version of success.

"Fans of the show 'The American Dream Project' will absolutely LOVE 'Success in Your City'," says Netflix's Chief Content Officer, Ted Sarandos. The show takes you inside the lives of an engaged couple that travels over 50,000 miles around America to discover the true meaning of success before they get married. They aren't just visiting these cities, they are living in them for a month or longer. Ted says, "This show is

unlike anything we have seen in a TV series, and I don't know how this couple pulled it off!"

December 27th, 2017, Brandon and Samantha set out on this journey to find the true meaning of success before tying the knot in marriage. Their first stop on the map was Scottsdale, AZ, where they learned from former 2-time MLB All-Star, Shea Hillenbrand, who played for the Boston Red Sox. Shea left baseball at the prime of his career with $20 million in the bank to pursue his childhood dream of owning a zoo. This dream soon became a reality, but four years later, Shea's property was foreclosed, his wife left him, and he found himself living out of his van. Shea hit rock bottom. On "Success in Your City," Shea shares his story of how he got out of his van and on to stages across North America speaking and helping other athletes transition out of sports.

While in Scottsdale, the "Success in Your City" team put on a fund-raiser for the Boys and Girls Club of Metro Phoenix and brought in the help of Kevin Harrington, the "Original Shark on ABC's Shark Tank." Kevin, Brandon, and Shea all spoke at the event and were auctioned off to bidders, which resulted in raising close to $40,000 for the Boys and Girls Club.

The success in Scottsdale put Brandon and Samantha off to a good start, but soon took a turn when they made their way to Austin, TX. With SXSW in town and other unexpected events, the couple found themselves living out of a hotel for a month with no vision for what to do next. Samantha says, "It was the most difficult obstacle we had encountered. We were stuck in a hotel with no vision, no funding, and down to our last hope for success." Brandon says, "Austin was our turning point. We almost quit! But we didn't. And I'm glad we didn't."

Within a few days after wanting to throw in the towel, they found support in Austin and captured the next success story featuring a couple in real estate who were taking a percentage of their profits from home sales and gave money back to families in need by renovating their homes. In this episode, the community comes together to renovate a home in 48 hours, just like you would see on the show "Extreme Makeover" with Ty Pennington.

Austin, TX, was a life-changing experience for the couple but this city gave them an entirely new perspective on life. They drove across the country to Boston, MA, where they met up with David France, the founder of Revolution of Hope, an orchestra for the youth in an under-served area. David moved to Boston 7 years prior with a vision to start his own orchestra. He didn't have much money, but he had the passion and drive to make it a reality. While pursuing his dream, David became homeless and slept on the streets of Boston. During the day, he had meetings with billionaires to get advice, and at night, he slept behind the Boston Aquarium.

Eventually, David was able to get 28 instruments donated, he found a location to play for free, and he recruited music teachers to donate their time helping kids learn how to play music. He created the orchestra literally from nothing. David is no longer living on the streets and frequently is flown around the world to speak and put on workshops for other youth musicians and entrepreneurs.

David's story changed the way that Brandon and Samantha viewed success and made them realize that you don't need material things to be happy. "You can do a lot with a little," says David France. After leaving Boston, they went back to their home in Iowa, sold 99% of their belongings and even sold their home, leaving them with no choice but to move ahead on their mission to redefine success.

Next on the map was Denver, CO, where they discovered women making a big impact on other women through fitness. Samantha specifically was interested because of her background as a personal trainer.

Prior to the "Success in Your City" tour, Samantha trained clients in gyms and taught classes online and offline.

While in Denver, Samantha started to wonder what her own version of success was. She knew that in order to find her own success, she would have to confront her past. Samantha's childhood at 13 years old was unlike that of most kids. Growing up, she was a gymnast who spent countless hours in the gym striving to be the best. One day, she lost her dream of becoming a star gymnast when she was introduced to drugs. At 13 years old, she was addicted to drugs and spent the next year living an uncontrollable life. Soon after quitting, she jumped into an 8-year abusive relationship. Samantha says, "I was a totally different person back then. Fitness is what helped me overcome my drug addiction and abusive relationship." In the Denver episode, Samantha, along with other women, share their difficult past experiences and how they are using their stories to drive their futures in the fitness industry.

The last stop on the map was Nashville, TN, known as the "City of Music," but also as the city where Brandon and Samantha planned to get married. While planning their wedding, they got to see what success meant to the country singer, Faydra Lagro, a Wisconsin native who moved to Nashville 3 years prior to pursue her dream of making it big in Nashville.

Brandon and Samantha have done things that most couples would only dream of, and they have experienced things that most will never get to experience in their lifetimes. But others will get to watch the entire journey of Brandon and Samantha this spring on Netflix.

"Success in Your City" is a 5-part series, along with behind-the-scenes content where the hosts and the entire team who created the show share what they learned and how they pulled off the show. You will be blown away by what happened behind the scenes to bring this show to life. You will never look at TV the same way again and it will forever change the way you view success.

Netflix said that they haven't quite seen a story like this before, nor have they partnered with a team like this before. Unlike most distribution deals, a media company pitches a pilot show to Netflix, and if Netflix gives the green light, they form a partnership to produce and distribute the show. Brandon and Samantha did the complete opposite. They self-funded and produced the show and showed up to Netflix headquarters with a plan to work together. They even sent a FedEx box prior to their arrival with a mock-up of them on the cover of "The Hollywood Reporter," and on the inside was a story of their partnership with them, exactly like the one you are reading now.

Netflix says, "They filmed their trip to our office too, believe it or not." Netflix subscribers will get to see this bonus footage and their journey to our headquarters in Los Gatos, CA. Netflix co-founder Reed Hastings, said, "At Netflix, we are creatives looking to provide a stellar experience for our customers and release content that changes the way you view shows. 'Success in Your City' does just that. We are excited to work together and bring this show to the masses."

"Success in Your City" has a powerhouse team who is working with Netflix to move forward to not only release Season 1 but also to start collaboration on Season 2 of the show. Their executive producers are Kevin Harrington "Original Shark on ABC's Shark Tank" and Jeff Hoffman "Co-founder of Priceline.com" who look to not only drive the success of this series but also to help drive the success of Netflix overall.

Their director is Shawn Vela, a 13X Emmy Award Winner who has worked on known documentaries with Jack Canfield, Peter Diamandis, Rudy Ruettiger and more. So far the Success in Your City series has won an Emmy for The Trailer of the Show and also an Emmy in the religion *category for The Shea Hillenbrand Story: Against All Odds. You can watch the trailer at SuccessinYourCity.com/RedefineSuccess.*

When I asked the couple what success meant to them, they said, "Success is helping others live their own version of success." Coming this spring they will be helping Netflix subscribers do just that.

When we look back at this article, we wonder if Netflix would have been impressed or angry by this mock-up. We have yet to find out the answer, but we certainly were thinking outside of the box. We had posted this on social media a few days prior to me going to their HQ in hopes of getting their attention. When we did post it, we pointed out that the article was a mock-up, not real—that it was our creative way of standing out. Even with that disclaimer, many people thought we actually had a deal with Netflix and were congratulating us and sharing the article to their pages. A few people cautioned us, thinking we might get in trouble with Netflix by performing the stunt we pulled because it was a "false advertisement." Society believes what it wants to believe, I guess. We never got in trouble, but the mock-up certainly got people's attention on social media.

A few days before I went to Netflix HQ, we received notification that our packages had arrived at both Netflix offices. I was going to show up at the Los Gatos location on Thursday, January 24, and then show up at the Los Angeles location on Friday, January 25. At each location we sent packages to specific people and prior to that, I had sent emails to some of them about my arrival. This entire process was thought out. I didn't just show up with no plan ahead of time. We did the best we could to set ourselves up for success to land this meeting on our own. At least we thought we did.

Wednesday, January 23, I boarded a plane at six thirty p.m. to leave Minneapolis. While on the plane, I felt excited and nervous. I couldn't believe that I was going to actually fly across the country with no meeting scheduled and just show up at Netflix with the mission to land a meeting. Part of me was questioning if I was making the right decision. It didn't matter anymore because there was no looking back. The packages were sent, I was on the plane, and I wasn't going back on what I said I was going to do. I had a layover in Dallas, which ended up being delayed, and then I finally made it to Sacramento around twelve thirty a.m. on Thursday. Once I landed, I rushed to the rent-a-car location, and luckily arrived just in time before it closed. Soon afterward, I started my drive to Los Gatos, home of Netflix HQ. At 4:07 a.m., I arrived at a friend's house in the city and got a few hours of sleep before the big "meeting." It was so hard to sleep, knowing that I had a potential chance to pitch our show to Netflix. Even if it was a 1 percent chance, it was still a chance.

That morning, I woke up at seven thirty a.m. and prepared for my "meeting." Before heading to Netflix HQ, I did a quick fifteen-minute call with my buddy Wes, who has been in the industry for years and produced and sold many shows to major networks including Netflix. He told me I was crazy but admired my courage and dedication. He said he thought there would be a slim chance of me getting past the front desk because everyone who comes into the HQ needs a scheduled meeting and point of contact . . . but he said if anyone could land the meeting, I could. For the pitch, he advised me to make it short and to the point and show my enthusiasm for the project. He said to sell the sizzle, not the steak. Basically, he meant to intrigue them and pique their interest, not try to share the entire background of the show.

After getting this encouragement and advice, I drove to Netflix. The first building I approached was closed due to renovation, so I ended up driving five minutes down the road. Once I got there, I put the car in park and took a few breaths. I was nervous and had no idea what to expect next. There was only one way to find out.

As I walked into the main doors of Netflix HQ, my heart started to race. A trophy case full of Emmy Awards faced me. At the front desk sat two girls and one said (and I'm paraphrasing all of this), "How can I help you?" I said, "I'm here to meet with so and so (we will keep their name confidential)." They said, "Do you have a meeting scheduled?" I said, "No, but they know I'm coming. They received a package from me a few days ago, and I had just emailed them." They said, "If you don't have a meeting, you won't be able to see them." I responded, "Is there anyone else in the unscripted TV show department that I can meet? I just traveled across the country to meet with someone." They responded, "No. Our answer doesn't change. You still won't be able to meet with anyone." I then said, "Well, can I sit over here and send them an email and let them know I'm here?" "Sure," they said.

I wasn't about to quit after hearing no from two people at the front desk. I'm not very good at hearing no. There is always a way to a yes! Within five minutes of sitting down, a security guard came down and asked me why I was at headquarters. I told him, and he said that I couldn't just show up looking for a meeting. He asked for my identification, which I happily gave him. He then started to walk me out the front door that I came in from. As he did, he got serious when he reiterated that I couldn't just show up like I had. "It's not the way things work," he told me. I expressed my passion behind our show and how much work we had put into it. I told him that we believed in our show a lot and that we believed it would be adding massive value to Netflix and its viewers. He didn't really care. He was just doing his job and wanted me to leave.

After concluding that I wasn't going to get anywhere with the security guard, I decided to go. Before I did, I shook the gentleman's hand, looked into his eyes, smiled, and said confidently, "I will see you again soon," as if I knew I would eventually get the meeting I had set out for.

As I walked to my car, I recorded an Instagram story to share what had just happened. I had actually recorded the entire trip up to that point to show others what I was doing, so they knew I was serious. It were as if everyone was watching the reality TV show of my life called *Brandon's Trip to Netflix*. I had more viewers on my Instagram story that week than I have ever had in my life. People were so intrigued by what might happen to me. They wondered if I would land the meeting or not. Suddenly after sharing my post, everyone was reaching out to me. Many people wanted to help, and some were starting to become trolls. Social media became crazy.

I headed to a local Starbucks, where I emailed the people I had planned on seeing at Netflix. I shared with them my story and that I was walked out of the office. While I sent these emails, I noticed my social media posts were gaining more traction and comments. Things were starting to get out of hand, and I started to question if I had done the right thing. I was starting to let others' negative opinions get to me.

Here are the comments (exactly as posted) from an Instagram post I made with a picture of the Netflix sign and with a message from me saying I tried to land a meeting with Netflix and wasn't going to quit:

"Ok, I saw ahead that you're coming to LA but why on earth would you go to the Los Gatos location. They handle the business of streaming service and have nothing to do with providing content. A google search of their job's website gave me that info. I work in this industry and you don't seem to have the skills to know where you should go so how or why would anyone take you seriously? This. Is. Not. How. You. Do. Things. In. This. Industry."

"We're triggered and creeped out someone would be this invasive. This is how to get blacklisted in the industry."

"Nope you're not doing anything right. And to be a 'hater' one would have to be jealous which for sure isn't the case lol Just watch-

ing to laugh at another entitled privileged white man thinking he's owed something."

"Lol those are NOT real Emmy's. Your sense of entitlement is unreal. It's really hard to do what you want to do. It doesn't just happen when you want it to. Millions of people who live in LA know that already. They are pursuing their shot in a way that isn't delusional or self-aggrandizing. I don't know who is encouraging this type of behavior in your life, but they are not helping you."

"In certain contexts, this sounds like you could be a straight up rapist, dude."

"I don't know you, but a friend of yours posted on a popular Facebook page asking for a contact for you at Netflix. This group is only comprised of woman. I was so sad to see so many slam your dreams, your drive, and ambition. The things they spoke about someone that they don't even know were hurtful to see, and all I could do was just pray for you and that God would bring the vision that is inside you to pass. I hope that everyone who doubted you and told you that your failure was certain will be humbled by your success. You have crazy faith in the vision and your faith will open big doors. Stay the course and be excited for what's coming. I look forward to seeing your work on major networks in the future and I pray you receive the desires of your heart. I apologize for all the woman who are basically stalking you on Facebook and Instagram and belittled your dream and drive. This is how you know you're on the right path. I'm rooting for you."

Many of these comments were brutal. I would be lying if I said that they didn't hurt me after reading them. They did, and they did make me question if my career in TV was over. The last comment, however, gave me hope. It made me not feel so bad after reading all the other negative comments. Over the years as I've gained followers and posted content on social media, I've had haters and I've had amazing fans. This post, by far, attracted the most hate I've received for one post. I don't wish bad things on the people who said those things to me. I pray for them and wish them the best. Usually, the people who put that hate into the world are the same people who have many troubles. What they put out in the world is what they are feeling on the inside.

I spent most of the day in that Starbucks in Los Gatos and received no emails back from Netflix. By the end of the day, I started my drive to Los Angeles to meet with other producers to get feedback about what I had just done. Many told me it wasn't the end of the world and that it was a great learning experience. I never did go to the Netflix office in Los Angeles, but I did keep emailing their executives, who to this day have yet to respond. I'm still emailing them, and I have emailed one person in particular twelve times. I'm persistent, and I know one day I will meet him and I'm confident we will laugh about it all. What follows is the first email I sent him the day Netflix sent me away from their HQ.

To keep the person's name confidential, we will use the name "Joe." Part of this email is edited because if I share with you all the detailed information about the person, you will be able to figure out who it is.

Hey Joe,

I admire you and what you have done to achieve your success. (Detailed information about a past job) You have worked hard and you deserve every bit of your success.

I've spent countless hours studying Netflix and the team building its future, including you.

In 2018, my wife and I traveled 50,000 miles across America, sold our house, and 99% of our belongings to go all in on the Mission to Discover the Truth about Success.

We filmed a TV series on it to change the way people view success.

I've traveled over 2,000 miles to land a 12-minute meeting with you. I also sent you a package last week that you should've received Tuesday.

I'm in LA tonight through Saturday morning to meet and share with you ways I can help you drive Netflix subscription growth and continue to retain current subscribers while also gathering more data for you to invest in the winners like "Stranger Things," "House of Cards," and "Black Mirror."

I appreciate your time and look forward to meeting you.

Best,

Brandon

P.S. Here is the trailer to our TV series which recently won an Emmy Award: SuccessinYourCity.com/RedefineSuccess

I don't regret showing up at Netflix. If I hadn't, I would be living with regret to this day. It was a valuable life lesson and experience. It allowed me to grow as a person because it forced me out of my comfort zone. Great things happen when you leave your comfort zone.

There are two main lessons I would like you to take away from my experience of showing up at Netflix.

Lesson Number One

You must always do what you think is right for you and go after something if you think you should. Don't let others' negative opinions or discouragement sway your decision. Do you. There will be times where you are faced with opportunities that may scare you, but don't let the fear hold you back. Face it, and you will realize the fear you build up in your head is way worse than what you actually experience while doing the thing that scares you.

Lesson Number Two

You should never say negative things to others on social media or target someone the way I was targeted. Try to put yourself in my shoes or in the shoes of any person who is being targeted on a post. Everyone has feelings, and everyone has their own problems. Be the person who puts out positivity into the world and lifts others up, not brings them down. Be like the person who didn't know me but took the time to write me a long comment that told me they were praying for me and wished me the best during my journey to achieve my dream. That small gesture that took ten minutes out of their day made the biggest impact on me and made my entire day. It shifted my energy and perspective on my current situation. Do good for others, or as our friend Joel Comm would say, "Do Good Stuff"!

Social media is a very powerful tool that can do a lot of good, but it can also be used to hurt others. It's time we all come together and ensure that we are the ones who don't allow negativity on social media. This negativity is what leads to depression and even suicide. In those few hours of reading those comments on my post, I felt like my world was coming to an end and that I had ruined my career overnight. They were just words. They were words that I let get to my head. Never again will I allow others' comments or negative energy toward me get to my head. I also encourage you to not let it get to yours. How often do we allow others' thoughts about us ruin our day or control our lives? As an entrepreneur, I've learned that you are going to always have haters and many people who will doubt you. Others will laugh at you and belittle your dreams. When you are striving to achieve something that no one has ever achieved, these things will certainly happen. Don't let anyone take away your dreams or goals. They are your dreams!

Chapter 16
Brandon

Where Would We Be If We Didn't Pursue Our Dreams?

Where would we be today if Thomas Edison had listened to negative people or criticism during his journey of creating electricity? I'm sure people thought he was absolutely crazy when he told them he would be able to create a way to power everything in your home and create the ability to have light without a fire or gas lamps. His invention has given us the ability to power everything we have and has made life simpler.

Where would we be today if Henry Ford had listened to negative people or criticism during his journey of making the Model T Ford automobile available to the masses? Most people probably told him he was crazy and that they could get a faster horse to travel from point A to point B. Henry thought outside the box and never quit until he achieved his chief definite aim in life, which was to create a faster and more commercialized way to travel. Henry has given us the ability to travel all around the country in a short period of time. He gave Samantha and me the ability to travel over 50,000 miles around the country in 2018 to pursue our own dreams and mission for this TV show. His accomplished dreams allowed us to accomplish ours. It becomes a domino effect.

Where would we be today if Steve Jobs had listened to negative people or criticism during his journey creating Apple with Steve Wozniak? Twenty years ago, I would have thought you were crazy if you had told me we would one day be able to see, clearly, someone on our phones thousands of miles away during a call. Just because I thought he was crazy doesn't mean I would ever belittle the man or his dreams. I'm glad Steve didn't allow the haters to get to him, because his work with Apple has completely changed our lives. Apple products have revolutionized the way we share art, music, TV shows, and talent with the world. It changes how we communicate with the world and our ability to share our experiences with others. Thank you, Steve Jobs!

During our journey of pursuing our dream and mission with *Success in Your City*, Samantha and I have had many haters and have been told we couldn't do what we set out to do. We have lost friends, followers, and have even had arguments with our loved ones. People laughed at us and told us we were wasting our time. While bringing this show and book to life, we have seen many obstacles that would have stopped most people from moving forward. We have faced bankruptcy from investing all of our money into our dream and being hit with other business hardships along the way. We almost called our wedding off due to tensions over the show and pursuing this mission of redefining success. We prayed together, cried together, and fought by each other's side, and we will continue to do that until the day we die. Nothing can stop us from chasing our dreams, and nothing should stop you either.

We have this one life to live, so why not live it to the fullest? Why not create great things in life and become unforgettable? Why not travel the country and film a TV show along the way?

When you have an idea or dream and someone tells you why you shouldn't do it, you should reply, "Why not?"

Anything is possible in the world we live in today. The individuals who go after their own versions of success and don't quit until they get it will be the ones who achieve success in business, life, and love. Those are the individuals who will live a much happier and fulfilled life.

Our hope for you is that you now have a better understanding of what success means to you in your life. Once you know what it is, it will be much easier to get there.

It will be a long road ahead, but it will be your own road to success.

Make it yours, and don't stop until you get what you are looking for. That is what success is all about!

The crazy ones who think they can change the world are the ones who actually do.

Go change the world and achieve the success you are looking for, because life is too short not to.

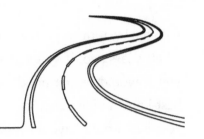

Afterthoughts from Brandon and Samantha

Brandon

There are so many forms of success, and only you can define what success means to you. As I look back on my twenty-nine years of life—my age as I write this book—and look back on the trip we took around the country, I notice that my perception of success is always changing. We all have different stages of success, and what you believe to be your success today could very well change a few years from now. You can only see so far into the future, and some of the amazing things that lie ahead will come at you in the most unexpected ways; and when they do, they will take you down a path that you would have never imagined. That path may alter your version of success.

Ten years ago, if you had asked me what success meant to me, I would have told you, "Becoming the richest man and best-known person in the ice business." Five years ago, if you had asked me what success was, I would have told you that it was be a multimillionaire with the best-known product on the market called Arctic Stick. Two and a half years ago, if you had asked me about success, I would have told you it would be me building the top media agency that produces the best-known video content in the world. Today if you ask me what success is, I would have a similar answer around creating the best-known video content and creating an award-winning show called *Success in Your City*. I would also tell you that success is being with the people I love, enjoying life to the fullest, helping as many people as possible, and becoming better every single day at what I do.

As you can see, the definition of success has changed for me several times over just ten years, from ages nineteen to twenty-nine. I wonder what my version of success will be when I'm thirty-nine or even sixty. We all are changing. Experiences, hardships, and highs and lows form us into different people and make our perceptions of life different. If I were to sum up what I've learned about success and what I've learned from everyone we spent time with in 2018, the following would be my answer about how to achieve your own version of success.

How to T.R.A.I.N for Success and Live Your Own Version of Success

1. **Take Action**—Your thoughts determine what you want in life, but action will determine what you get. Many people will dream up the greatest aspirations and ideas, but only a small percentage of them will act toward achieving them. The ones who follow through will eventually find their success. David France dreamed to create an orchestra, and he committed himself to making it a reality. He focused on it and took the necessary steps to achieve it. He asked people to join him. He attended meetings to gain more knowledge. He asked others to donate toward the cause. He did everything he could to make his dreams become a

reality. He took action! If you want to achieve anything worthy, you will need to act to achieve it.

2. **Relationships Are Key**—The people you regularly surround yourself with will ultimately define who you become and what you achieve. These relationships will decide how happy or unhappy you will be: your relationships with your significant other, family, friends, mentors, business associates, business partners, clients, and audience. The people who are around you can positively or negatively influence your life. Be around people who have the same aspirations and are supportive of you and your endeavors. If you are around people who are negative toward you or try to shut down your ideas or dreams, you will never achieve the big things you dream of. Get negativity out of your life and be around positive people. Build relationships with people who want to help you achieve your own version of success.

3. **Add Value**—Always add value to others. Add value to your wife or husband. Add value to your family and friends. Add value to your business associates and clients. Heck, I'm adding value to everyone I come in contact with, which can be as simple as smiling at someone, giving them a compliment, or encouraging the Uber driver to go and read the book *Think and Grow Rich* by Napoleon Hill. Real estate gurus Ricky and KodiKay Cain have added massive value to their clients in Austin by helping them buy and sell their homes with ease. That value they added led them to amass lifelong customers. It led them to go from having an office in a closet to becoming one of the top real estate teams in Texas. They also add value to their community through their nonprofit, Cain Cares, helping renovate homes in need. This not only helps the people in need, it is also raises the value of the

real estate in the community. The moral of the story is that the amount of value you add to the world will decide how much value will come back to you.

4. **Invest in Yourself and Your Future**—Always invest your time, money, and resources into your own self-development and your future. You get out of something what you put into it. Faydra Lagro invested in herself and her future at a young age. She practiced music all through elementary school, middle school, and high school. Despite her teacher's advice, she went to college for music, which allowed her to become more knowledgeable in her line of work. While at college, she joined a band that allowed her to continue to invest her time in music, which, as a result, gave her more experience and credibility. The ultimate investment for her was making the leap to move to Nashville and go all in on her career. She made music her sole income, besides serving at bars, which led her to gain relationships with the people who booked musicians to play at bars. These relationships led to her playing at the bars and gaining more exposure. Every move that Faydra made was all in service of developing her career as a full-time musician. Because of that, she has played at bars almost nightly on Broadway, she has an EP out, and she will get exposure from this book and our TV show. Her investment has paid off for her and will continue to pay off as she moves forward.

5. **Never Give Up**—You can't beat someone who never quits. Life is going to throw curveballs at you and is going to test you in so many ways. Many times you will want to give up and throw in the towel. The easy route would be to do just that. Shea Hillenbrand played baseball for years—years of persistence and hard work—before he got his chance at the major leagues. He became

a two-time All-Star who was at the top of his game and made $20 million in the process. After leaving baseball, he was tested once again with a foreclosure of his zoo and his wife leaving him, resulting in him living out of a van. He almost committed suicide, but after hitting this all-time low, he found God. He saw that he could still thrive. This led him to meet the woman of his dreams who he is happily married to today. It led to him speaking at churches, prisons, and in front of kids. It led him to pursue his passion for helping others through his nonprofit, Against All Odds. Shea has been at the top of the mountain, back down to the bottom, and to the top again. Life is a rollercoaster ride and the only way to make it to the top in life or achieve anything you desire is to never quit. You just have to keep going!

These are the five key steps that have allowed me, Samantha, and many others to achieve our own versions of success in business, life, and love. I promise you that if you follow these steps, you will achieve your goals. Follow them, apply them, live them, breathe them, and make them your laws of life. I look forward to seeing where your road to success takes you. Here's to your success!

Samantha

A lot of people look at other people's lives and assume they are okay. Okay in a way that they don't struggle and that their smile signals that they are happy. Throughout the year of our travels for the show, I definitely glued a smile on my face a lot of the time. I wanted to hide the depression. Hide the fact that it was one of the hardest years of my life. I held everything in to avoid others questioning me.

Truthfully, I wasn't okay. I was in a lot of pain emotionally. I felt suffocated because I didn't know how we were going to pull everything off. Most of the time, we were barely getting by. Many times, all of this stress put me in a negative mindset. That's what my year of travel did. I went from being newly engaged, ready for our next chapter, to wanting to call off the wedding and leave that life behind me. I piled on so much resentment toward Brandon that it made me question everything. I know his heart was trying to guide me to complete the show and to live with an open mind, but man was he testing me. Working with my future husband seemed ideal at first, but after the struggles we endured, I felt that our relationship suffered because he didn't know when he needed to treat me as a wife or as a business partner.

In a way, I felt I was playing a part that wasn't aligned with who I really was. I just wanted to get through the year without failing. I was consumed with what needed to be done, so I forced myself into doing whatever that was, even if that meant putting my happiness to the side. Not every day was bad. I had a lot of wins, but I do wish I would have enjoyed more of what was right in front of us instead of worrying about the unknown. Now, I have many memories that I will cherish and friendships I have gained, but I still felt like a lost soul for most of the year.

Was I alone? Probably not. But because I didn't express my feelings to the outside world, that is how I felt. Because I stayed silent, I lost out on a lot of potential memories. Above all the hardship, I am a stronger person because of it. I now have an open mind. I have a relationship with God. I don't worry as much. Most importantly, I have learned to do what is in my heart instead of doing what I feel others would like to see me do. I've grown so much, and I continue to strive to work toward doing things that make me happy. My success is being happy with what I'm doing in life. I don't want to build my life off of other people's judgment. I just simply want to be happy with what I'm doing.

I've had many takeaways from exploring other people's definitions of success, and I hope you can look into your life and, in your own way, use what I've learned.

First, the value of time—we are not promised time. We must live knowing that our time can end at any moment. Using our time for the things that make us happy has been something that I continue to work on. I feel that many people, including myself sometimes, don't see the gift that is in time. We were given this incredible life to use our gifts to help others and to make the world better. We often overthink what it is we need to do in this world when what we need to do is quite simple: Be kind, do something you love every single day, surround yourself with people who lift you up, and most importantly, take care of the only body you have.

Another incredible thing about time is spending it with others. My time with the kids at the Boys and Girls Club made me realize that they just wanted my time of day. They didn't care about materialistic things. They wanted to play and talk to me about what they liked to do at the club. It was eye-opening, as I've mentioned before, to know that me just being there was enough.

Money does not promise happiness. Boy did I have this wrong. I used to see success as having unlimited money, a mansion, a couple of cars, and endless trips to the spa to improve my appearance. The world we live in defines success as exactly that, when in reality it has nothing to do with the amount of money we have. Some of the richest people in the world do not have happiness. They continue to chase after money, and they forget to simply live. Throughout the year, I took away a huge lesson: Money does not always bring you the life you want. Yes, it can help you do good for others, but if you are overconsuming materialistic things, you will have a lower chance of feeling truly happy because what you have will never be enough.

Always do what's in your heart. I don't mean always do what's in your head. Your heart. Go for what you want for yourself, not what you feel you should do to please the outside people in your life. For many years, I lived my life based on trying to "fit in." I still have not cracked this completely, but I have discovered that when I show up in a way for myself, I can show up in other areas of my life in a more positive way. I don't spend as much energy on being down on myself for trying to prove myself to everyone. The most important relationship we have is with ourselves. We need to do what's best for us so we can use what fuels us to help others find that light as well.

Gratitude made my life better. I had never written down what I'm grateful for until after the Austin episode. Speaking with KodiKay and Brandon and me finding our faith were gifts that were given to me and because of that, my perspective on life is forever changed. In the midst of me thinking that my world was ending, I wasn't looking around at what I did have. My health. A shelter. Eyesight. The support of our team. I continually looked at what we didn't have and consequently, I suffered from a lot of unnecessary pain. There is so much good in our lives, and we sometimes—if not often—overlook it. We always want more. I don't go a day without speaking out loud what I'm grateful for. This has changed my perspective on what life is actually about. I get to live. No matter how hard life may seem at times, I always look at what good there is in the situation and I focus on that.

These are my thoughts and the important points that I have learned from exploring what success means. I hope you can look at your own life and dig into what it is that drives you to be the person you truly want to be.

BONUS Chapters

Bonus Chapter: Kevin Harrington—Why Failure Is a Necessary Lesson
Bonus Chapter: Shawn Vela—Your Story Is Your Success
You can access Shawn's chapter at
SuccessinYourCity.com/TheRoadtoSuccessBonus

Success in Your City **TV Series**

You can find out where to watch our TV series at SuccessinYourCity. com. If you are interested in having us speak at your next event, email us at Contact@SuccessinYourCity.com.

Follow us on social media at the handle @SuccessinYourCityShow and also follow our hashtags #SuccessinYourCity and #ThisIsSuccess.

Follow Brandon T. Adams @BrandonTAdams.

Follow Samantha Rossin @SamanthaJRossin.

If you would like to join our Success Mastermind where we help others achieve their own version of success, go to SuccessinYourCity. com/SuccessMastermind.

As for season two, that's up to you! We are looking for stories to share and places to visit during our next adventure. If you want to be a part of our mission in redefining the meaning of success, email us at Contact@SuccessinYourCity.com.

If you have a story that you think we need to share, reach out to us.

We look forward to coming to a city near you in 2020 and beyond.

Kevin Harrington on Why Failure Is a Necessary Lesson

The first time I was a salesman knocking on doors, I was fifteen. I had started a driveway-sealing business. I'll never forget the very first time I went out into a neighborhood to sell my services. It was a nice neighborhood with homes that were about eight to ten years old with driveways that were the same age. In Cincinnati, my hometown, the winters would get cold and put cracks in those driveways. As I knocked on doors, I heard no, no thanks. No thanks. No thanks. I knocked on literally twenty doors and didn't make any sales. Some people were like, "Hey, sorry. I'm at dinner. I'm not interested." I got the door slammed in my face many times!

What I learned then is that "no" indicated that these people were the decision makers. Well, I decided to not take "no" for an answer—that I would help them make a different decision. I came up with a strategy, the seed of which had been planted in a question many of these potential customers had asked me: Had I done any jobs in the neighborhood? My answer: No. So then they asked me what I was doing in the neighborhood then, and I told them that my sister lived there—which was true. So they asked me if I had sealed her driveway. I said no again. They told me to come back after I did hers. So, I sealed her driveway. Then I put a sign in her yard that told everyone I had done the work, and I had before and after pictures to prove it. Wow, did that ever work miracles. Afterward, I went from door to door in that same neighborhood and closed probably fifteen of those driveway sales. Pretty amazing.

By changing my sales strategy, I had given my sister's neighbors a better reason to give me a chance at a yes. Their previous "no" had told me that if they could make a decision that quick with a no, they could make a decision that quick with a yes. You just have to turn it around. Getting that no was a decision-making process. The lessons I learned as a driveway-sealing salesman in my teenage years taught me a lot about life and being an entrepreneur. Hearing no doesn't mean it's a no-go. It's feedback from your customer that you need to improve your product or improve your pitch.

Today, I speak all around the world and share my forty years of entrepreneurial experience with others to help them achieve their own success and ensure that they don't make the same mistakes I did over the years. I've had some ups and downs, but I've learned from those mistakes and sometimes more from those mistakes than from my successes. In different talks, I use the quote from Winston Churchill that goes, "Success is being able to go from failure to failure without the loss of enthusiasm." I did not always have that attitude, but the more sophisticated I became, the more I realized that hey, I'm going to get up today, do my best, and may still fail. If I fail, I want to fail fast, fail cheap, and get to the winners. I want to focus on the winners.

What I learned is that failing would make me smarter, better, and when the winner hits, I'd know what to do. So, in the old days in my business of airing infomercials, we'd bomb a product launch. We'd bomb another product launch, and it would fail miserably. We'd have seven or eight launches in a row that would bomb. We were like wow, are we out of business? Are we ready to close up shop? What do we do?

Then suddenly, our next product launch was a huge winner. When we launched Tony Little's Gazelle, it did hundreds of millions of dollars in sales. Having that major win made us realize that we had to endure failures to get to that major success. A lot of people just don't understand that failure is part of the whole process. They fail, and they are like, I'm out, I'm done; but failure is just the beginning. Failure is always giving you valuable feedback and lessons that can help you become better at what you are doing and get you closer to that huge win.

Now that I've been through enough failures and losses in my career, I don't get so worked up about them. I now get to mentor my own son Brian, who works with me. After getting out of college, Brian worked in the corporate world for a while and then he came to work with me. He joined me in the *As Seen on TV* space, and we owned AsSeenonTV. com and As Seen on TV Inc. He would get all excited when someone would walk in and pitch us a new product. He would be like, "Dad, this is going to be a home run! Here is our next hundred-million-dollar product!" We would invest in the product and start bringing it to market. We would spend sixty days getting the contract, then we would get the contract. Then we would spend sixty more days manufacturing the product and another sixty days shooting the commercial and the infomercial. We would hire talent for the shoot and go all out. We'd have $200,000 and more than six months of our lives invested in the project.

We would test it, and it would bomb. "Is it dead?" Brian would ask. He'd say, "I don't understand. I thought this was going to be the biggest winner we ever had." Brian was so devastated when something that he really thought was going to work didn't. He put his blood, sweat, and tears into everything and was counting on it to be a success, then it would bomb. I would be like, "Brian, you got to shake it off, man. You're only going to hit them one out of three or one out of four times." That's the reality. Now, I'm a seasoned guy. I've been in business for more than forty years, so I don't let things shake me. When things fail, that means the market is telling me it's not going to work. Don't let a failure ruin your life. But also, that's why you have to tweak your idea because maybe you went about it with the wrong pitch, the wrong approach, the wrong this or the wrong that. The bottom line is that you have to mentally prepare yourself for what could happen if things don't work out.

When trying to achieve success, you also have to surround yourself with the right people who can help you get through those failures and obstacles, because you don't know what's going to happen along the way. If Brian had been on his own trying to do all this stuff, he might have just given up and been like, "Wow, this is way too tough and I'm never going to be able to do this." But me, I'm always sitting here saying, "Brian, look. Don't let this define who you are and make you think that you are picking losers. Let's go pick five more, and if we do six or seven, we may have two or three winners out of those. We started with one failure, but let's not give up!"

Not all of your ideas are going to be winners. Everyone thinks their product is going to be the next big thing, but only the market can decide that, not the person with the idea. I always remember when people would call me and say, "Hey, I saw you on *Shark Tank*. You invested in this deal! That's a piece of crap! Mine's a thousand times better than that!" Everyone believes they've got the next home run, the grand slam. But guess what? They don't necessarily. They are probably going to fail their first few times. They are probably going to lose. That's just how business goes. I had to condition my mind to deal with failure because that's part of life. Do I quit? Do I give up? No! We learn from failure. We take the best things that we can from what we learn to tweak our ideas and make something that will work. Also, just because something tested soft doesn't mean it will be a complete failure; it means that we may need to try a different approach.

When we first put Tony Little on the air with the Gazelle, it bombed and everyone was like, "Wait a minute. This is the Gazelle! This is walking on air, and this should be huge. This is a grand slam product!" We would ask ourselves what we did wrong. We analyzed the product and features. We first thought maybe the product was too expensive. Then we thought maybe the product made people think it was just for fit people like Tony Little, who looked like a body builder. So, we decided to have fun with it and show people that this product was for everyone. We filmed infomercials with young and old people, male and female, using the machine. We changed up the presentation and aired the info-mercial a second time. We increased the sales, and they rose by almost 100 percent. In the second airing, we did the same thing. We tweaked the infomercial, brought it back a third time, and brought up our sales another 50 to 75 percent. By the fourth airing, we quadrupled the success of the first airing. Now, this product was on the Home Shopping Network (HSN). Now, we had a home run! Again, just because something doesn't test successfully the first time doesn't mean it's a failure. You've got to tweak, tweak, tweak. This is part of the process of finding your home run.

I have had plenty of projects that we tweaked and tweaked and tweaked, and we still couldn't get their sales up. Those are the products you need to drop; and that is the time to move on to the next one. That's where Winston Churchill's quote comes in. Be able to deal with failure after failure without losing enthusiasm. If something is a failure, then it's done. Get it out of here, and move on to the next one. That's the mindset you need to have in business to succeed. You are going to have a lot of failures on your journey to success.

You are probably wondering at what point you should make another tweak or make a pivot and move on to the next product. When we test a product, we use ratios. I'm in a business that's defined by numbers and ratios. If I spend $10,000 in media, and it does $5,000 in sales, it's a bomb. But we then tweak it. If I tweak it and take it from $5,000 to $10,000 in sales with $10,000 in media spend, now I have what I call a 1 to 1. I'm still not making money, but I'm moving up the chain. Before, I was at a .5 to 1, which is a half—$5,000 in sales on $10,000 in media. On a 1 to 1, I'm still not making money because the media was $10,000 and the sales were $10,000, but I still got to buy the product and ship the product. We tweak again, and if we take it to $20,000 in sales on the third tweak, that means we are making a great progression going from $5,000 to $10,000, to now $20,000 from only $10,000 in media spend. We are now at a 2 to 1 ratio and over the hump. Now, our product is making money. It's not a grand slam, but we just quadrupled our sales and got something that's making a small profit at 2 to 1.

In the world of infomercials, TV media, and in *As Seen on TV*, the threshold that we look for is a 2 to 1—a 2 to 1 sales to media ratio. Now, a winner is a 3 to 1 or a 4 to 1. The Gazelle may have started out at a .5 to 1, then went to a 1 to 1, then to a 2 to 1, then to a 3 to 1—and that's when we went to the monster rollout. If you are tweaking and spending $10,000 in media and doing $5,000 in sales, and you tweak things and are still at $5,000 in sales, and you tweak it and you go to $6,000 in sales, you're not gaining enough to get to 2 to 1. You have to see significant gains. This is how we work it. This would be the same thing if you were doing Facebook ads or Instagram ads to sell a product. If you are spending $5,000 or $10,000, you want to see a multiple on that ratio.

When we first tested the product called Peeps, an eyeglass cleaner, it was doing a 4 to 1 on Facebook, Instagram, and other media. For $5,000 in media, it was doing $20,000 to $25,000 in sales. At $100,000 per week in media, it was still doing $400,000 in sales. That's when we knew we had a grand slam. That's how you roll it out. That's what you are looking for, and when you get a ratio like that, you know you have something that's working. Peeps has now gone on to sell 2.5 million units and has done more than $100 million in revenue. It's a home run product!

In the early days of my business, we would do all types of projects looking for our next big home run. We would try new categories. We would go to a houseware show and try a blender or a mixer. Then we found the George Foreman Grill, and that took off like crazy. Then we found the Chinese Woks, and they took off like crazy. We started exploring different categories we had never done before. We tried knife sets. We did the Ginsu knife set, and that worked well. We never knew that fitness was going to work, but we started doing fitness products that helped you get abs and that worked. The more things we tried, the more successes we had. Each failure would tell us what we shouldn't be doing and would direct us to all the things we should be doing. It only took one major product launch to make up for all the losers, but you have to come across enough losers to get to that winner.

I would take products to the shopping channel and if something didn't work the first time, they would say, "Kevin, don't let it ruin your life. You got four airings today. Go back to the drawing board! You just got back at seven a.m. on the first one, but you are on again at eleven a.m. for your next one. Go back to the drawing board, watch the video of the live appearance, and tell us what you think you did wrong. Let's improve this. We are going to make this a lot better." It's not won and done. Tony Little usually didn't have a major hit the first time he went on air with a product. We would put him on HSN and QVC. His first airing would generally be very soft on almost any product that he would pitch. He never really let that kill him after he became a little more seasoned because he realized that was just the first time.

When you are going out to the marketplace, a million other people are out there. They are going to give you feedback and ask questions. We used the HSN market to develop our pitch. People would call in and ask specific questions about the Gazelle, about what it could specifically do. Those questions made Tony realize he needed to better explain to the audience how to use the product. He would incorporate that into his next pitch because he realized if they were asking questions about things that he thought they understood but they didn't, he needed to cater to those questions in his pitch so the audience would understand the product. He learned from that and how to do the pitch as he was actually doing the pitch, which gave him feedback from people. This is similar to crowdfunding today. Crowdfunding is feeling the pulse from the market and finding out if people like your idea or your product. Are they willing to pre-purchase it? The crowd will decide, and their feedback is very valuable.

Tony would go on an infomercial with twenty minutes to pitch. Sometimes in the first four minutes, virtually nothing would happen: no phone calls, no orders, nothing at all. Then suddenly, somebody would call in and say something that others would identify with. Boom! The phone lines would start lighting up. What that person would say showed us in real time what everyone else was thinking. The next time we aired, we put that question in at the two-minute mark instead of minute eight. As we were developing all these things, we were learning the pitch as we went. That's how you develop a quality pitch!

Pitching is a skill you will need in all aspects of your life, not just business. We are always trying to convince someone to do something in our favor. We are always selling someone on a product, an idea, or an outcome that is in our favor. The better your pitch is, the better the results you will get. The only way to master your pitch is by trial and error and hearing the word no. It's by getting feedback from the marketplace. The only way to get to that point is to experience many failures and many losses along the way. Failure is a lesson to learn from that will get you closer to your successes. You just need to keep pushing forward. It hurts, and there are real implications about what it does to us personally, but it can also be used as a lesson.

If I had quit when I heard my first "no" knocking on doors as a kid, I wouldn't have learned the valuable lesson that comes with no. If I hadn't worked through that no, I would have never got into the infomercial business and selling products. If I had quit on my first few product launch failures, I would have never got to the grand slams like the Gazelle, Ginsu knives, Chinese Woks, or Peeps. These grand slams ultimately led me to gain the experience and branding necessary to land me on the TV show *Shark Tank*. *Shark Tank* changed my life and has allowed me to share the stage with amazing people all over the country and mentor many amazing entrepreneurs like Brandon T. Adams and Samantha Rossin.

Brandon and Samantha have also come to understand the powerful lessons learned through failure. When they were stuck in a hotel in Austin, Texas, for a month and down to their last dollars, they kept going and were rewarded just days later. Most people would have quit. Most people would have thrown in the towel, but they didn't. They kept going toward their own success. They got in their car and kept driving on the road to their next city. They had many ups and downs and overcame many obstacles along the way. Their perseverance and never giving up led to our team winning two Emmy Awards, filming season one of *Success in Your City*, and bringing an amazing show to you to help you achieve your own version of success.

The lesson to learn here: You can learn from failure. Failure is necessary in life. Without it, you will never find your grand slams. Embrace failure, and use it to propel you forward, not hold you back. You've got to prepare your mind for it. What is Winston Churchill telling you? Success is being able to go from failure to failure without losing your enthusiasm. Don't let it take you down! Be prepared to fail, because that's part of life.

About the Authors

Brandon T. Adams is an Emmy Award-winning producer and co-host of *Success in Your City*, a TV series on a mission to redefine the meaning of success. Brandon is a keynote speaker, podcaster, producer, and author and the publisher of the magazine *Accelerant* in 2017-2018. He is also the associate producer and youngest featured entrepreneur in the movie *Think and Grow Rich: The Legacy*, which is based off the classical bestselling book *Think and Grow Rich* by Napoleon Hill.

Samantha Rossin is an Emmy Award-winning producer and co-host of *Success in Your City*, a TV series on a mission to redefine the meaning of success. Samantha is also on a mission to help women find the courage to discover happier and healthier versions of themselves. She is a fitness expert who loves spending time in the gym and helping other women with their fitness goals online. Samantha was born in Winona, Minnesota, and visits regularly to spend time with her family.

Brandon and Samantha currently reside in Minneapolis.

CPSIA information can be obtained
at www.ICGtesting.com
Printed in the USA
JSHW010327310820
7544JS00003B/39